THE POCKET IDIOT'S GUIDE TO

The ASVAB

by Laura Stradley and Robin Kavanagh
Figures by Kara LaFrance

ALPHA

A member of Penguin Group (USA) Inc.

ALPHA BOOKS

Published by the Penguin Group

Penguin Group (USA) Inc., 375 Hudson Street, New York, New York 10014, USA

Penguin Group (Canada), 90 Eglinton Avenue East, Suite 700, Toronto, Ontario M4P 2Y3, Canada (a division of Pearson Penguin Canada Inc.)

Penguin Books Ltd., 80 Strand, London WC2R 0RL, England

Penguin Ireland, 25 St. Stephen's Green, Dublin 2, Ireland (a division of Penguin Books Ltd.)

Penguin Group (Australia), 250 Camberwell Road, Camberwell, Victoria 3124, Australia (a division of Pearson Australia Group Pty. Ltd.)

Penguin Books India Pvt. Ltd., 11 Community Centre, Panchsheel Park, New Delhi—110 017, India

Penguin Group (NZ), 67 Apollo Drive, Rosedale, North Shore, Auckland 1311, New Zealand (a division of Pearson New Zealand Ltd.)

Penguin Books (South Africa) (Pty.) Ltd., 24 Sturdee Avenue, Rosebank, Johannesburg 2196, South Africa

Penguin Books Ltd., Registered Offices: 80 Strand, London WC2R 0RL, England

International Standard Book Number: 978-1-59257-982-2
Library of Congress Catalog Card Number: 2009928404

12 11 10   8 7 6 5 4 3

Interpretation of the printing code: The rightmost number of the first series of numbers is the year of the book's printing; the rightmost number of the second series of numbers is the number of the book's printing. For example, a printing code of 09-1 shows that the first printing occurred in 2009.

Printed in the United States of America

Note: This publication contains the opinions and ideas of its authors. It is intended to provide helpful and informative material on the subject matter covered. It is sold with the understanding that the authors and publisher are not engaged in rendering professional services in the book. If the reader requires personal assistance or advice, a competent professional should be consulted.

The authors and publisher specifically disclaim any responsibility for any liability, loss, or risk, personal or otherwise, which is incurred as a consequence, directly or indirectly, of the use and application of any of the contents of this book.

Most Alpha books are available at special quantity discounts for bulk purchases for sales promotions, premiums, fund-raising, or educational use. Special books, or book excerpts, can also be created to fit specific needs.

For details, write: Special Markets, Alpha Books, 375 Hudson Street, New York, NY 10014.

Contents

Introduction

Congratulations! By deciding to join the United States Armed Services, you've decided to pursue one of the most honorable and fulfilling lines of work in the world. There will be no punching a clock from 9 to 5 for you. You crave the challenge of pushing your physical and mental boundaries. The thrill of the hunt. The camaraderie of your brothers- and sisters-in-arms.

But before you can get there, you have to make it through recruitment. The military wants to ensure that those it takes into its ranks will be able to succeed, both personally and professionally—which is why you have to take the Armed Services Vocational Aptitude Battery (ASVAB from here on out).

Since you've picked up this book, you're already showing that you've got what it takes to make it in the military. Rule no. 1 is that you don't do anything without good intel. What we've compiled for you is a quick and easy-to-read guide that will help you get shipshape for the ASVAB in no time.

How to Use This Book

We've designed *The Pocket Idiot's Guide to the ASVAB* to give you a good sense of what the test is all about, why you have to take it, how it's broken down, and how to get the scores you need.

The first three chapters give you an overview of the test itself and how you should approach and prepare for the ASVAB. This information is probably the most important in the book. If you read nothing else, make sure you get these chapters in.

The remainder of the book details what you'll find on each subtest, what you need to practice and look out for, and strategies for choosing the right answer. You also get sample questions and answers/explanations so you can put all of our great advice into practice.

Extras

Along the way, be sure to look for these power-packed extras:

def•i•ni•tion

These mini-lessons give you a better understanding of terms you'll hear a lot during the recruiting process and give you a better understanding of the ASVAB in general.

Heads-Up

These little facts and hints help you steer clear of trouble on the exam and give you the info you need to make smart decisions about your future.

Test Tip

These are quick and effective ways to increase your ASVAB scores and plan for your career ahead.

Classified Intel

These are fun facts about the test, those who've taken it, how it's used, and other tidbits to help keep things in perspective.

Now that you've got the lay of the land, it's time to get to work. Hup to it!

Acknowledgments

From Robin Kavanagh:

Special thanks to Keri Cerami, for her mathematical brilliance; Tom Kavanagh for his awesome automotive knowledge; Wendy Mamilovich, who helped an old friend; Petty Officer Albert Scales; Ken Pecharsky; Marilyn Allen; and everyone who contributed their experiences and tips. And of course, thank you to our team of fabulous editors: Randy Ladenheim-Gil, Lynn Northrup, Janette Lynn, and David Jordan.

Special Thanks to the Technical Reviewer

The Pocket Idiot's Guide to the ASVAB was reviewed by an expert who double-checked the accuracy of what you'll learn here, to help us ensure that this book gives you everything you need to know about preparing for and taking the ASVAB. Special thanks are extended to David Jordan.

David Jordan grew up all around the world in an Army family and is currently a graduate student and teaching assistant at MIT, where he studies mathematics.

Trademarks

All terms mentioned in this book that are known to be or are suspected of being trademarks or service marks have been appropriately capitalized. Alpha Books and Penguin Group (USA) Inc. cannot attest to the accuracy of this information. Use of a term in this book should not be regarded as affecting the validity of any trademark or service mark.

Chapter 1

Basic Training

In This Chapter

- All about recruitment
- What the ASVAB is and why it matters
- How to approach the test
- The ASVAB and your career choices

You may be thinking that your days of tests and studying are far behind you because you're looking toward the military for your future. Think again. Throughout your years of service, you will be getting a nearly constant education by acquiring new skills either through training school or out in the field.

With each new hurdle you attempt to jump, you will be tested on your knowledge and ability. The U.S. military wants to get an idea of your current level of education and skill before making the decision to allow you entrance. That's where the ASVAB comes in.

In this chapter, we give you the back story on the ASVAB, why you have to take it, what it tells the military, and how it can help you choose the career that fits you best, both while you serve and afterward. But first you need to learn what to expect from the recruiting process.

Looking for a Few Good Men and Women

The U.S. Armed Forces are always looking for new faces. Though the draft is still technically on the books, it has not been used since the Vietnam War. Throughout the military actions that have taken place since then, our volunteer Army, Navy, Marine Corps, Coast Guard, and Air Force have served and protected our shores and interests worldwide.

Recruiters play an essential role in maintaining these numbers. Though there are certainly times when interest in enlistment peaks—for example, the years since the terrorist attacks of September 11, 2001—it's a recruiter's job to actively seek out those who might be interested in a life of service and place them where they're needed most and most likely will excel.

The Recruitment Process

People find their way into a recruiter's office in various ways. Perhaps a friend or family member joined up and encouraged them to check it out, a recruiter visited their school during a career fair, or they answered a specific ad on a job website.

However you connected with your recruiter, here are some of the steps to enlistment you can expect to go through:

1. **General questions:** When you first meet your recruiter, he or she will try to get a sense of whether you qualify for that specific branch of the military. The recruiter will ask you about your health and drug history, physical appearance (whether you have tattoos, piercings, etc.), interests, goals, and more.

2. **Education history:** Your level of education determines your overall eligibility and what *Armed Forces Qualifying Test (AFQT)* scores you need to hit for entrance (check out Chapter 2 for more on this). For example, those who have passed the General Educational Development (GED) test may have to score higher than those who have a high school diploma to be eligible for entry into some branches of the military. Some branches do not accept GEDs.

3. **Take the ASVAB:** You'll either go to a Military Entrance Processing Station (MEPS) or a Military Entrance Test (MET) site to take the test. The outcome of your ASVAB determines how you will move throughout the rest of the recruiting process. When your recruiter gets your scores, he or she will begin to formulate career advice and options. You'll discuss these after the results of your other tests come through.

def•i•ni•tion

The **Armed Forces Qualifying Test (AFQT)** is actually comprised of the two verbal and two math subtests of today's ASVAB. The scores on these sections are calculated, scaled, and compared to a sample group of test takers of the same age range and demographic as you. This final score is the one that determines enlistment eligibility.

4. **Physical and psychological examinations:** Basics like blood pressure, height/weight, vision, and hearing are tested and recorded. Expect blood and drug screenings, and possible strength or stamina tests.

5. **Moral character assessment:** This test also takes place at a MEPS location. This may include extended interviews, credit and criminal background checks, and even a financial history. Requirements for this vary.

6. **Career counseling:** If you've made it to this point in the process, chances are pretty good that there's a place for you in the branch of service you've chosen. You haven't signed a contract yet, though. This interview with your recruiter walks you through your job options based on all your test results.

After you've gone through all these steps, you'll get an offer from the military stating what your job will be, how much you'll be compensated, and the time of service you'll be responsible for fulfilling (among other things). Make sure that you read the contract carefully and that you agree to all of what's stated before signing.

You're under no obligation to any branch of the military until you sign an official contract offer. You can change your mind throughout any stage of the process until that point.

Once the Contract Is Signed

Congratulations! You're the newest member of the U.S. Armed Forces. Exciting, isn't it? Before you start packing your duffel bag and enlisting someone to look after your car while you're away, keep in mind that you may not be sent into active duty right away. Only a small portion of new enlistees are expected to begin their service within a month of signing their contract. The rest are enrolled in the *Delayed Entry Program (DEP)* and are assigned a date on which they have to report for duty.

def•i•ni•tion

The **Delayed Entry Program (DEP)** was designed to control the number of new enlistees that are assigned to training schools by giving them specific dates they will begin active duty. Those in the DEP can wait up to a year, although the average wait time is four months.

If exceptional circumstances arise, you can ask for your active duty date to be pushed back up to an additional year, even if you've been delayed for a full year already. Some high school students can also apply for DEP status so that they can graduate before beginning their service.

How Does the ASVAB Fit In?

Taking the ASVAB is the most important step in recruitment: without the right AFQT score, you're not eligible to join any branch of the military.

Imagine you are the owner of a successful auto body shop and are in need of a new mechanic. Thousands of applicants respond to your "Help Wanted" ad. How do you select the best person for the job? You wouldn't want to choose someone who'd never handled a wrench, would you?

The same is true for the military. There's a long-standing (figurative) help-wanted sign hanging from the shingles of recruiting offices all around the country. Each of the Armed Forces is always looking for men and women with skill, talent, drive, and honor to join their ranks.

The ASVAB is a standardized exam given to all potential military entrants. (A slightly different version is also administered to some high school students as a career-counseling tool.) It determines not only entrance eligibility, but also eligibility for certain training schools and jobs within the military and, in some cases, signing bonuses (cha-ching!).

You're given a series of 8–10 tests, depending on which version you take. We discuss this more in Chapter 2. For now, just know you'll be tested on the following:

- Vocabulary
- Reading comprehension
- High school math and reasoning skills
- Basic science
- Ability to assess spatial relationships
- Mechanical principles and knowledge
- Understanding of electronic systems and components
- Automotive and general shop knowledge

Today's ASVAB is the result of painstaking and methodical research, adjustment to changing time and needs, and exacting standards to ensure as fair and accurate an assessment as possible.

Why You Need to Ace the ASVAB

The thought of having to sit for hours and answer question after question on subjects that may or may not apply to your areas of interest may not be the happiest in your head right now. We get it, which is why we're offering you a new way to look at taking the ASVAB.

The way we see it, taking the ASVAB is a huge opportunity for you to learn something about yourself in general. Simply sitting through the exam doesn't obligate you to enter the service. If you choose to enter the military, your test scores will determine whether you're eligible for acceptance and what jobs you are allowed to train for.

However, if you decide the military isn't for you, you can use your scores to figure out what you'd like to do next. You can assess what you're good at and what you're not, whether those areas in which you excel gel with your interests, or whether you've just opened new areas to explore. You'll be able to determine whether continuing your education is a good idea and where to focus your studies.

Knowing all this, it's a good idea to try to get the highest score possible on every section of the test. This will give you the best look at your abilities overall.

Chapter 2

Essential ASVAB Intel

In This Chapter

- Taking a closer look at the ASVAB
- Understanding your score
- Comparing the paper versus computer test
- Devising your best test-taking strategy

You wouldn't run a race without spending weeks getting your body in shape. You'd risk falling on your face in front of a huge audience—or, worse, pooping out before reaching the finish line.

The same applies to the ASVAB, except that you won't be gasping for breath and clutching your side after going through our workouts—and you'll earn a better payoff. A little brain power and some time are all you need.

This chapter gives you the rundown on how the ASVAB is structured and administered and how to use this information to develop strategies that will translate into higher scores.

Up Close and Personal

The smart way to train your brain is to get up close and personal with the test itself: how it's sectioned, how many questions are in each part, and how much time you have to answer them.

A little knowledge goes a long way on any standardized test, it's not so much the subject matter that you're being tested on—it's more about how you take the test itself.

The Armed Forces Qualifying Test (AFQT)

If you thought you avoided the joys of math and verbal questions by not taking the SAT or ACT, think again. To be accepted into any branch of the Armed Forces, you have to get a minimum score on the Armed Forces Qualifying Test (AFQT), which is all about math and verbal skills.

The AFQT is divided into four sections:

- Word Knowledge (WK)
- Paragraph Comprehension (PC)
- Mathematics Knowledge (MK)
- Arithmetic Reasoning (AR)

The Word Knowledge questions (see Chapter 4) test you on your vocabulary. Though this section is pretty straightforward, the sooner you start studying, the greater your vocabulary will be come test time.

In the Paragraph Comprehension section (see Chapter 5), you read short paragraphs and answer questions based on what you read. It sounds easy, but questions here can be tricky if you don't know what to look for in an answer.

The Arithmetic Reasoning section (see Chapter 6) asks you to go beyond simple equations, which also makes it a bit more challenging. What's tested here is your ability to reason (as the name suggests), apply logic, and follow through on each step of a word problem to get the right answer.

The Mathematics Knowledge section (see Chapter 7) tests you on basic grammar and high school math skills. Don't worry if you're rusty on your algebra and geometry. Some review and practice will get you back on track in no time.

For now, you should know that the minimum *percentile scores* you need for the branch of service you're applying can range from 30 to 60. These standards are subject to change. Always check with your recruiter for up-to-date score requirements.

def•i•ni•tion

A **percentile score** tells you how you did in comparison to a sample portion of others who took the test during a sample period. For example, if your score report places you in the 90th percentile, only about 10 percent of test takers in a fixed sample scored higher on the overall AFQT than you did.

The Military Occupational Specialty (MOS) Tests

Unlike with the AFQT, how you perform on the Military Occupational Specialty (MOS) tests does not affect your entrance eligibility. It does, however, determine what career path options are open to you because the Military Occupational Specialties are jobs that require a specified amount of knowledge and skill. For example, you have to show a high aptitude in science, math, and electronics to qualify for a job that focuses on electronics.

Each branch of the military requires minimum scores on certain subtests in order to qualify for MOS jobs. Don't be surprised, though, if your composite scores indicate that you'd be great in a variety of occupations. Sometimes seeing what your strengths are in black-and-white can open up a whole world of possibilities you've never thought of.

The good news about this part of the ASVAB is that you don't have to go nuts trying to cram all sorts of information into your brain. These subtests are based on general knowledge that any high school graduate or GED holder would know.

Here are the sections of the test:

- General Science (GE)
- Electronics Information (EI)
- Automotive and Shop Information (AS)
- Mechanical Comprehension (MC)
- Assembling Objects (AO)

The General Science section (see Chapter 8) tests you on the basics of physical, earth, and life sciences. Don't worry if you slept through bio; brushing up should be enough to get you through this part of the test.

In Electronics Information (see Chapter 9), you'll find all sorts of questions about electrical systems, components, circuitry, terminology, and other technical basics.

Automotive and Shop Information (see Chapter 10) is where your industrial arts classes and weekends working on your car pay off. You get to strut your stuff about all things related to cars, tools, and hardware.

Mechanical Comprehension (see Chapter 11) is mostly about physical science, how machines work, and how mechanical principles apply in real life.

Finally, Assembling Objects (see Chapter 12) focuses on perception of spatial relationships based on illustrations.

Score Explanations

All ASVAB questions are scored as either a 0 or a 1. However, this doesn't mean that each question is worth the same. Scaled ASVAB scores are based on Item Response Theory, which takes into consideration several factors:

- Assigned difficulty of questions
- How a question discriminates among those at different levels of ability

- The likelihood that a guess from a test taker with a low level of ability will result in a correct answer

This is the reason two people can take the ASVAB, get the same number of questions correct, and come back with differing scores.

When you get your scores, you'll see several numbers on the page: standard scores, composite scores, and AFQT percentile scores.

Standard scores, also known as line scores, are given for each of the AFQT and MOS subtests. They can be anywhere between 0 and 100, based on the number of questions you answered correctly. On the ASVAB, you're not penalized for a wrong answer; you just don't get any points for it.

Composite scores determine your MOS eligibility. They're divided into four branches of the military: Army, Air Force, Navy/Coast Guard, and Marines. The scores are broken down into subcategories specific to the types of jobs offered in each branch. They are also calculated differently depending on the area of service.

The AFQT Percentile is the final score at the bottom of the report. It shows how your standard scores place in relation to a sample of recruits who have already taken the AFQT. This score determines your eligibility to enlist.

Wikipedia has a good sample ASVAB score report that you can look at to see how yours would look: go to http://en.wikipedia.org/wiki/ASVAB#Composite_scores.

The Two Faces of the ASVAB

When you go to your local recruiting office, they may have you take an ASVAB-like test there. Sometimes they'll give you a test sheet and a No. 2 pencil and tell you to have at it. Other times, they'll sit you in front of a computer that will shoot questions at you one by one.

Classified Intel

Coast Guard recruiters don't offer in-office pre-testing. When asked why, Petty Officer Albert Scales said it's just something that has never been part of their recruiting process.

When your recruiter feels you're ready, you'll go to a Military Entrance Processing Station (MEPS) to take the real ASVAB. Larger MEPS sites provide "one-stop shopping" for military recruits. Often your recruiter will accompany you there, and you also may be scheduled to complete some of the other entrance tests, such as physical or psychological evaluations.

If you don't live near one of the 65 MEPS sites throughout the country and Puerto Rico, you will have to take your test at a Military Entrance Test (MET) site, which could be a federal office or building, a reserves center, or even an armory in the area.

Your options of which version of test you can take may be limited, depending on where you take the exam. The Computer Adaptive Test (CAT) is becoming the most frequent way to administer the test. CAT versions of the ASVAB offer test takers an alternative to the traditional fill-in-the-bubble paper test. Basically, you deal with only one question at a time, record your answers electronically, and get your score at the end of the test.

At sites where CAT is available, you may not have the option to take a paper version of the ASVAB. So it's a good idea to learn exactly what each version is like and the pros and cons of each.

The Computer Adaptive Test (CAT)

With the CAT test, the difficulty of the questions you are presented adapt to how you answer the ones before. Your first question will be at a medium difficulty level. If you get it right, the next question will be harder. If you got that question wrong, the next one will be easier. Keep in mind that you *want* to answer hard questions. They will help get your scaled score up.

Try to get as many questions correct as you can in the beginning of the test. If you start out with a high score, maintaining it is a lot easier than trying to build it up from a lower one.

What if the mere thought of looking at a computer monitor wipes your brain clean? Don't worry! Every testing site gives very detailed and easy-to-follow directions and training on how to take the computerized test. There are also safeguards that give you a second chance to consider your answer before making it final. As long as you can move a mouse and click a button, the CAT will be no problem for you.

There are some differences between the CAT and paper ASVAB, other than how you record your answers. The biggest is the number of questions you have and how much time you are given to answer them. The following table shows how the CAT ASVAB is broken up.

Computer Adaptive Test ASVAB Sections and Times

Subject	Number of Questions	Minutes
General Science (GS)	16	8
Arithmetic Reasoning (AR)	16	39
Word Knowledge (WK)	16	8
Paragraph Comprehension (PC)	11	22
Mathematics Knowledge (MK)	16	20
Electronics Information (EI)	16	8
Auto Information (AS)*	11	7
Shop Information (AS)*	11	6
Mechanical Comprehension (MC)	16	20
Assembling Objects (AO)	16	16
Total	**145**	**154**

*The Auto Information and Shop Information scores are presented under one label: AS

When you're done with one section, you simply move on to the next. Because you're not waiting for the allotted time to run out on every section and you have fewer questions to complete, the average test taker completes the CAT version of the ASVAB in about an hour and a half. However, you can't go back and review your answers. Once you submit a final answer, there's no changing it.

You also may find that scheduling a CAT ASVAB is much more flexible. Since a proctor (someone who administers the test) is not needed, you don't have to wait for a full class to be formed in order to schedule your exam.

The Traditional Paper and Pencil (PAP) Test

If you've ever taken a traditional standardized test in your life, the paper and pencil (PAP) version of the ASVAB holds no surprises for you.

First, you'll be given both test booklets and answer sheets. A proctor will oversee checking everyone into the testing session and give instructions on what you are to do and when. Sure, this may be just a preview of what you'll experience in basic training, but following these instructions to the letter is always a good idea. A proctor who is not obeyed is a cranky proctor.

After administrative duties are taken care of, the test begins. The following table shows how the PAP ASVAB is broken up.

Paper and Pencil ASVAB Sections and Times

Subject	Number of Questions	Minutes
General Science (GS)	25	11
Arithmetic Reasoning (AR)	30	36
Word Knowledge (WK)	35	11
Paragraph Comprehension (RC)	15	13
Mathematics Knowledge (MK)	25	24
Electronics Information (EI)	20	9
Auto and Shop Information (AS)	25	11
Mechanical Comprehension (MC)	25	19
Assembling Objects (AO)	25	15
Total	**225**	**149**

When you're finished with a section, you can go back and review questions and answers in that section *only*. You have to wait until time is called, and then you can start the next subtest. When all is said and done, expect the PAP to take three or four hours. Your scores will be sent to your recruiter in a few days.

Scheduling a PAP ASVAB may be more restrictive than a CAT because of the administration of the test. A proctor must be present to handle all the paperwork and maintain a controlled environment. PAP versions are also frequently given at MET sites, where personnel may be sparse. Often a whole group of recruits must be assembled before a test date is assigned, which makes availability unpredictable.

> **Test Tip**
>
> No matter which version of the test you take, always answer every question. Unanswered questions on the CAT result in a penalty. On the PAP, you have nothing to lose, so making educated guesses is an easy way to pick up some extra points.

CAT and PAP Head-to-Head

Now that you know a little about what both versions of the ASVAB are like, it's time to look at the pros and cons of each:

Computer Adaptive Test

Pros:

- The test takes less time and has fewer questions.
- The test adjusts to your skill level.
- You get your results immediately after you finish the test.
- You have more flexible scheduling options.
- You can leave when you're done.

Cons:

- The test may not be available at every testing center.

- You have to answer every question you're given, in the order it's given.

- You can't change an answer once you finalize it.

- If you don't answer a question, you'll receive a score penalty.

Traditional Paper Version

Pros:

- You can jump around within a single section of the test and play to your strengths more easily.

- You can go back over questions in a section or change your answers if you have time at the end of a subtest.

- The paper test may be more comfortable for those more familiar with this type of format.

- You can skip questions and not receive a score penalty.

Cons:

- There's room for error in marking your answers on a form that has bubbles to fill in.

- You have to wait for days to get your results.

- Scheduling options are not as flexible.

- You have to wait the allotted time for each section to run out before you can move on to the next.

Knowledge is Power

By now, you've got a good idea of what you'll face when you sit down to take the ASVAB. But how can you use this knowledge to increase your score and reach your career goals?

Talk with your recruiter so you can get an idea of what type of career you want to pursue and the MOS scores needed to qualify for that training. This will help you concentrate on scoring well in the areas most important to your interests and future.

Try to take the test at a facility that offers the type of format you're most comfortable with. If there isn't one near you, focus only on strategies that will familiarize you with the format available.

Use the information about time limits and numbers of questions per section in your practice sections. It's great to know the right answer to a question, but if you run out of time before you get to answer it, you won't get the points.

Chapter

3

Strategies for Success

In This Chapter

- Using test-taking strategies
- Choosing the best answer
- Making an educated guess
- Practicing for the ASVAB
- Getting ready for the actual test

Throughout most of our school years, we're often told that we can't really "study" for a standardized test. This may have been true back when you were required to take only a handful of these types of tests over your whole education, but not anymore.

Today many states require almost annual assessments of academic ability through tests given to all students. The result is that teachers all over the country are essentially teaching students to pass the test—and not much else because government funding often depends on how well students score.

"Teaching to the test," however, covers only the content that may be tested. It doesn't break down the questions and give you the tools you need to find the right answer. This chapter walks you through effective strategies for taking the ASVAB that you can apply to nearly any multiple-choice exam (which you'll have your fair share of once you're in the service).

Rethink Your Test-Taking Approach

When you were given tests in school, you probably were asked to answer a variety of question types. Fill-in-the-blank, short answer, essays, true/false— all of these types have one thing in common. They require you to come up with the whole answer all by yourself, and that's the end of your chance to get credit for the question.

The cool thing about tests like the ASVAB is that all the correct answers are right in front of you. The trick is figuring out which answer to choose. This is actually a lot easier than you might think, if you adjust the way you approach taking the exam in the first place.

Step 1: Answer the Question on Your Own

Multiple-choice exams are essentially a guessing game, and the best way to win is to know what you're looking for before you ever look at the answer choices.

Start by making sure that you read the directions and your question very carefully before deciding on a likely answer. Under time constraints, test takers often rush through the question, come up with a quick answer, and end up missing crucial information in the question itself that will lead them to the correct answer.

Take your time and make sure you fully understand what the question is asking before formulating your own answer.

Step 2: Look for the "Best" Answer

Most standardized questions don't ask you to choose the *right* answer; they ask you to find the *best* answer out of the four choices you're given. Chances are, your answer is a lot better. But your task is to find the choice that will get you the points.

This is all part of the test design strategy. Those who write these exams want to see that you not only can come up with the correct answer, but also can recognize its varying forms.

They also have to be very careful about how their answer choices are worded so that there are very definite reasons one is the better than all the rest. This works to your advantage as a test taker because you can look for specific things to eliminate incorrect answer choices.

Step 3: Use the Process of Elimination

When you know what you're looking for, go through the answer choices you're given to figure out which one you should choose. If you think about it, it makes more sense to look for answers that are wrong, simply because there are more of them.

Some choices will obviously not be what you're looking for, but others will give you pause. This is where having an answer in mind will help you the most.

Use this information and eliminate the choices that don't fit your criteria. If you can get your odds down from one correct answer out of four to one correct answer out of two, your chances of selecting the correct letter go way up.

Heads-Up

Always go through all the answer choices before making your selection, even if you're 100 percent sure your answer is right. This will help minimize mistakes.

This works for most questions you'll see on the ASVAB, although math is often an exception (we get into specific ways to attack math answer choices in Chapters 6 and 7).

Step 4: Mark Your Answer Choice Carefully

This may seem like the easy part, but marking the answer you choose for a particular question can be tricky. The problem is that, no matter how right your choice may be, there is a margin of error in getting the answer in your brain onto the paper (or computer).

With the paper and pencil (PAP) test, you have an answer sheet on which you need to fill in very small bubbles that are packed closely together. Filling in the right bubble on the wrong line is very common. Check and double-check that you are filling in the right bubble in the right space for the question you're answering.

If you're taking the Computer Adaptive Test (CAT), you don't have to worry about filling in the wrong bubble because you can answer only one question at a time. Do be careful that you choose the right letter of the choice you're looking to mark, though.

Use your scrap paper to write down the answer choices and cross off the ones you want to eliminate. Circle the one that you believe is correct; then check and double-check that it's the answer you're selecting on-screen. Once you make your selection, you'll be prompted to confirm that this is your choice. Take this opportunity to check again. Better safe than sorry.

Test Tip

Make use of the test booklet (which you can write on) or scratch paper you're given during the test. Writing down your thoughts, taking notes, or even making lists of A-B-C-D so that you can check off which answer choices you don't need can be an invaluable way to work through questions, especially if you learn best by both seeing and doing.

Putting It Together

Now that you know how to approach your test questions, let's try out the steps on a General Science question. For now, just read the following question and don't look at the answer choices:

> The upper chambers of the heart are the atria, while the lower chambers are called the:

Step 1: Your first task is to figure out what the chambers of the heart are called. They are atria and ventricles. The question tells us that the atria are the upper chambers. Logic tells us that the lower ones must be the ventricles.

Step 2: We know we're going to look for the best answer out of the four answer choices. So let's take a look at what they are and see which one matches our answer:

A. Adenoids

B. Valves

C. Aorta

D. Ventricles

Step 3: Right off the bat, you can eliminate choices A and C, since they in no way resemble the answer you came up with. (And if you didn't know this, adenoids are located between your nose and throat. The aorta, which is related to the heart, is the largest artery in the human body.)

We're left with two answer choices that sound similar and both have to do with the heart. This is where you may start to second-guess yourself. Answer choice D matches the answer you came up with, but because you know the heart has valves and you're looking for an answer that is plural and begins with a *v*, you may wonder if your first instinct was correct.

If you are absolutely sure that "ventricles" is the correct answer, this is the one you'd choose (and you'd be right). If you weren't 100 percent sure, take a good look at the question and the answers.

The question is asking about chambers of the heart. What do chambers do? They are places where things are kept. A room is a chamber. The answer you're looking for describes something that is like a room.

Even if you don't know what a ventricle is, you probably know what a valve is: something that enables and/or prevents a substance (usually liquid) from going from one place to another. Your kitchen faucet is a valve.

Which of these two answers is the better match for a word that describes a chamber or room? By eliminating "valves" as a possibility, you come up with the correct answer: ventricles.

The Educated Guess

Another great thing about the ASVAB is that you're not penalized for wrong answers—you simply don't get credit for them. This makes guessing a good idea throughout the test because you have nothing to lose and everything to gain.

Even if you don't know the answer to the question, you can eliminate answer choices that you know are not correct and then make an *educated guess*.

def•i•ni•tion

An **educated guess** is one you make based on some kind of logic or using information that you have to make a reasonable guess about which answer to choose. It's always best to make an educated guess instead of a random one because it increases your chances of getting the question correct.

Eliminating answers that you know are not right is a great way to start making your educated guess.

Even if you have no idea what the question is asking, chances are you can eliminate at least some of the answers and up the odds in your favor.

Here are some specific things to look for in answer choices that are telltale signs that they're not the best answer.

Extremes or Absolutes

ASVAB test writers like to keep things neutral. If an answer choice has words that indicate some type of condition that is too far to one side or another, chances are this is not what you're looking for. Watch out for words like *never, always, furious, enraged, overjoyed,* or anything else that hints at absolutes or extreme emotion.

The exception to this is in the Word Knowledge section. Sometimes you'll have to find a synonym for an extreme word, like *egregious* (which means "extraordinarily bad"). In this case, you'll need to look for an answer choice that is equally extreme. If you had both "bad" and "horrible" in your answers, you'd want to choose the latter.

Contradictory Information

Many times, particularly in the verbal sections, answer choices directly contradict the information given in the question, information you're asked to read, or even another answer choice.

If an answer choice goes against what's in the question or passage, that's a dead giveaway that the choice is most likely wrong. However, if an answer choice contradicts one of the other choices, this is a signal to spend some time here to figure out which one is your best bet.

Similarities

When you see two answers that are very close in meaning, it's easy to get stuck trying to figure out whether there's a trap there. Generally, when this happens, neither answer is correct and the only thing you gain is more time passed on the clock.

If your instincts are telling you that there's something there, see what other answer choices you can eliminate. Then come back to those and look for specific reasons you think one might be correct. In most cases, you'll find the correct answer elsewhere.

Test Tip

Be flexible when it comes to your answers because choices you're given may not match up with what you were thinking. When this happens, try thinking about the question and your answer from a different perspective.

Practice Makes Perfect

In the military, your drill sergeant will tell you that the best way to get better at push-ups is to do push-ups—not bench presses, not weight lifting, but push-ups. Likewise, the best way to get better at the ASVAB is to take practice ASVABs.

You need to do two essential things when you prepare for the ASVAB. The first is to refresh yourself on the subjects and topics you'll be tested on. The second thing is to test your knowledge by answering practice questions. Not only will this enable you to practice the techniques we've outlined for you and exercise your brain on the material you've been studying, but it will also calm your nerves, boost your confidence, and enable you to do your best on the real thing.

Set Up a Routine

To effectively study for the ASVAB, you need time. Schedule a little time every day over a few weeks to work on your ASVAB skills. Thirty minutes to an hour per day is a good place to start.

Make sure that you …

- Choose a place where you're comfortable and where you'll be undisturbed. Someplace where there's no phone or computer is best.

- Leave the rest of your hectic life behind. Don't let any other worries or concerns about other aspects of your life take precedence.

- Have everything you need close at hand.

Don't beat yourself up for missing a study session or two. Try to adjust your routine if you need to, or sneak in some extra study time later.

Take It Step by Step

The ASVAB is a big test, and it can seem overwhelming. The easiest way to approach preparing for such a huge undertaking is to break it down into smaller parts—subtests, perhaps (as outlined in Chapter 2).

When you're making out your study routine, try to focus on only one subtest at a time. This will help you keep your mind concentrated in one area and increase your chances of retention. Also, if you've determined that you want to focus on only specific subtests for the job you're aiming for, this will save you a lot of time. Study those sections and work on those practice questions, and you can be sure you're making the best use of your study time.

Timing Is Everything

Just about everything in the military is timed, and for good reason. If you respond slowly to an emergency situation, lives can be lost or security breached. That's why—whether it's securing your gas mask, getting to work, or drawing your weapon—you're constantly racing the clock.

The same holds true for the ASVAB. Taking timed practice tests is essential, especially if you're the type of person who gets nervous with timed tests.

The more you practice at home, the better you'll be able to pace yourself and keep yourself cool and on-target.

Test Tip

Recruiters are there to help and can be one of your greatest assets when preparing for the ASVAB. Don't be afraid to ask for help.

Getting Ready for the Real Thing

As the date of your actual ASVAB nears, you can do a few things to make sure you're in the best shape possible:

- **Schedule some R&R.** A day or so before the test, try to ease up on the preparation. This will give your brain a chance to rest so that it's in top shape on test day. Also, the entire week before the exam, try to get as much sleep as you can.

- **Eat up.** Have a little something packed with protein the morning of the test. This will help keep your blood sugar up and hunger at bay.

- **Pack up.** Make sure you have everything you need for the exam with you and ready to go. Find out from your recruiter the type of identification and other specifics you'll need, as well as what you can't bring to the site.

- **Arrive early.** Make sure you're there at least 15 minutes before the test begins, to take care of any administrative business and ensure that you get the seat you want. Traffic and unforeseen events are not excuses for being late to the test, so allow yourself ample time.

Finally, if you're not feeling well, have a fever, or have recently gone through a stressful or emotional event (good or bad), your test scores may not accurately reflect your abilities. Remember that you can always reschedule the test if you think your life circumstances will impact your results.

Word Knowledge Defined

In This Chapter

- Why you're tested on this
- Types of questions you'll see
- Techniques for choosing the best answer
- Vocabulary-building tips
- Practice questions, answers, and explanations

The Word Knowledge (WK) section of the ASVAB is basically a big vocabulary test, only better. If you remember the ones you had in high school, all you probably got was a list of words you had to define.

Not so with the ASVAB. With four answers to choose from, context clues, and our expert test tips, the Word Knowledge subtest could possibly be the easiest vocab test you've ever taken.

This chapter shows you what types of questions you can expect to see on the Word Knowledge subtest, how to approach the questions, what to look for, and how to narrow your chances of figuring out the correct answer even when you don't know what the words mean.

Why Do I Have to Take This?

The Word Knowledge subtest is not really about how good your vocabulary is. It's more about determining where your communication skills are at. Believe it or not, writing and communication are essential skills for all military personnel.

Between studying in training school, writing reports for your instructor or commanding officer, drafting memos and e-mails, and completing any number of other administrative tasks, you need to be able to communicate clearly and efficiently. This starts with a good vocabulary. You don't need to know every word you're going to be tested on, be able to write out complete definitions, and use them in sentences. The ASVAB is looking to test your understanding of the words, how they're used in context, and their general meaning.

Types of Questions

On the PAP version of the ASVAB, you'll only have 11 minutes to answer 35 of these questions. On the CAT, you'll have 8 minutes to answer 16 questions. You'll encounter two types of questions on the Word Knowledge section of the ASVAB—and they both test you on *synonyms*.

Each has its pros and its cons, as well as tricks to help you choose the answer that will get you the points, even when you have no idea what the word means.

def•i•ni•tion

> **Synonyms** are words that have the same general meaning.

While the four-step process we outlined in Chapter 3 is definitely the best way to approach these questions, you can use specific techniques to help narrow your answer choices that apply only to this section.

Simple Definition

These are very straightforward and ask you to choose the answer choice that most nearly matches the meaning of the word given. If you don't know what that word or one of the answer choices means, there are lots of ways you can narrow your answer choices and get some kind of clue to the word's meaning:

- **Find the root:** If you're familiar with Greek and Latin word roots, prefixes, and suffixes (which we get into later in this chapter), you'll be able to get a general idea about a word's definition. For example, if you encounter the word *anachronistic*, you can break it down by its roots:

  The prefix *an* means "against."

  The root *chron* means "time."

  The suffix *ist/ism* can mean "action or process."

You can reasonably conclude that anachronistic has something to do with a process or an action that goes against time.

- **Positive or negative:** Prefixes and suffixes can give you a good idea about whether the word you're looking at is a positive or a negative. The correct answer choice will be on the same side as the word in the question.

- **Part of speech:** The correct answer choice will be the same part of speech as the word in the question. If you know that the word you're given is a noun, you can eliminate any answer choice that is not a noun.

Words in Context

These are sentences with a single word underlined. Your job is to choose the answer choice that gives the meaning of how the word is used in the sentence.

Heads-Up

Be careful with synonyms in context questions. Many words you'll find on the ASVAB have multiple definitions. Read the sentence carefully to see which definition applies to the word and how it works in that specific sentence.

While you can still apply the same techniques you would for simple definition questions, here are

some additional strategies to help you attack these
questions:

- **Look for clues:** More often than not, definite clues in the sentence will lead you to
  the meaning of the word. Look for specific
  words that modify or apply to the underlined
  word. Then when you go to the answer
  choices, look for one that matches the clues
  in the sentence. Look for clues in the following example:

  The rainy day had turned Mark's energetic
  mood into something more <u>lackluster</u>.

  Some words that give you an indication of
  what lackluster means include "rainy day,"
  "turned," "energetic mood." What happens
  to our moods when it rains? We can get
  depressed or lose energy. What effect is the
  rain having on Mark? The sentence tells us
  that he was full of energy, but the rain has
  changed that. So the answer we're looking
  for is the opposite of "energetic."

Test Tip

If you look at the construction of a word,
you can sometimes see smaller words
within that hint at the definition. The previous example uses the word *lackluster*,
which means "dull." The word *luster*, when
it stands alone, means "shiny." Add *lack* to
that, and you have a totally different (but
logical) meaning.

- **Swap it out:** A great way to approach a context question is to swap out the answer choices for the underlined word. This will help you eliminate a good number of wrong answers. Try it here:

Usually creative and vibrant with his writing, the student unexpectedly turned in a <u>prosaic</u> essay that only stated the facts about his topic.

(A) old

(B) abandoned

(C) boring

(D) luxurious

When you replace "prosaic" with the answer choices, you're left with this:

Usually creative and vibrant with his writing, the student turned in a <u>old</u> essay that only stated the facts about his topic.

Usually creative and vibrant with his writing, the student turned in a <u>abandoned</u> essay that only stated the facts about his topic.

Usually creative and vibrant with his writing, the student turned in a <u>boring</u> essay that only stated the facts about his topic.

Usually creative and vibrant with his writing, the student turned in a <u>luxurious</u> essay that only stated the facts about his topic.

Of all the answer choices, C is the best choice. "Abandoned" and "luxurious" really don't have anything to do with writing an essay and can be easily eliminated. Though the student could have turned in an "old" essay, our context clues of "usually creative and vibrant in his writing," "unexpectedly," and "only stated the facts," suggests that the correct answer will refer to how the essay is written, not its age.

Build Your Vocabulary

In addition to learning how to approach the questions in the Word Knowledge section of the ASVAB, it's a good idea to start building your general vocabulary. A couple of words each day can go a long way toward raising your score.

Hit the Books

Most libraries have a section devoted to test preparation, and here you'll find vocabulary guides. Use these books to make a list of words you want to learn, and work on learning them a few at a time over a couple of weeks. While you're there, pick up some light reading as well. The more you read, the more your vocabulary grows.

Memorize in Clusters

Many of the words you'll likely encounter on the ASVAB have similar meanings. For example, *florid, embellished, bombastic, ornate, overblown, flowery,* and *elaborate* all have similar meanings: "excessively decorated, spoken, or written." Use a good thesaurus and make out a list of synonyms for any vocabulary word on your list.

Learn Your Roots

We talked earlier about being able to recognize prefixes, suffixes, and word roots. This is an invaluable tool for improving your vocabulary because it gives you the tools for understanding how words are built—which, in turn, clues you into their meaning.

Test Tip

Check out www.prefixsuffix.com for an extensive list of word roots that you can access for free and use to memorize these ancient building blocks.

Some common roots include …

- **a/ab/an/:** Away from, without
- **acy/cy (suffix):** Noun, state
- **ary/ar (suffix):** Adjective, relating
- **anti/de:** Against, away from, opposite
- **bene:** Good
- **beli/bel/pug:** Fight, war
- **circ:** Around
- **chron:** Time
- **com/con:** With, fully, together
- **dic/dict/dit/loqu/locut/log:** Speak
- **inter:** Between

- **intra:** Within
- **luc/lum/lun/lus:** Light
- **mal:** Bad
- **omni:** All, ever
- **spec/spic/vid/vis:** See
- **viv/vita/vivi:** Life

Make Associations

One of the easiest and most lasting ways to learn
new words is to associate their meanings with
something that makes sense to you. You may come
up with a little rhyme or word associations that
remind you of the meaning. We call these mnemonic devices, and as long as they make sense to
you, they can consist of just about anything. Here
are a few to get you started:

- **Pretentious:** Pretends to be all that
- **Miser:** Scrooge was a miserable miser
- **Levity:** Levitates your mood
- **Concrete:** Hard evidence
- **Intrepid:** Bold, gutsy, like the famous air-
  craft carrier

Classified Intel

You can subscribe to word-of-the-day websites
that will e-mail you a new vocabulary word and
definition every day. Typing "word of the day"
into your favorite search engine should net lots
of options.

Practice Questions

Now that you have the tools for working through Word Knowledge questions, it's time to practice your technique. For each of the following questions, select the answer choice that most nearly means the same as the underlined word.

1. Implacable most nearly means

    (A) merciful.

    (B) unbending.

    (C) joyous.

    (D) intelligent.

2. Raucous most nearly means

    (A) raspy.

    (B) quiet.

    (C) expected.

    (D) scandalize.

3. The opulent house had expensive antiques and famous paintings in nearly every room.

    (A) dirty

    (B) empty

    (C) transparent

    (D) luxurious

4. After having traveled nonstop for 24 hours, she felt ragtag until she showered and changed in her hotel.

    (A) unkempt

    (B) beautiful

(C) vivacious

(D) shredded

5. <u>Florid</u> most nearly means

(A) inept.

(B) gorgeous.

(C) embellished.

(D) natural.

Answers and Explanations

1. **B.** The prefix *im* means "not" and *plac* means "please." So the answer we're looking for is a negative or something that suggests not pleasing someone. "Unbending" is the only answer choice that suggests an act that does not please.

2. **A.** "Raspy," "quiet," and "expected" are all adjectives. The *ous* suffix in "raucous" tells us that the word is an adjective, so we can eliminate "scandalize" because it is a verb. A good way to remember the definition for *raucous* is to associate it with the phrase "rowdy ruckus," which implies some type of loud disruption. "Quiet" is opposite of this definition, and "expected" has nothing to do with sound. Answer A, "raspy," is the best answer.

3. **D.** The context clues in this sentence point to an answer that has to do with wealth and money. "Luxurious" is the only answer choice that makes that connection.

4. **A.** How would you feel after traveling for 24 hours straight? Probably pretty grungy, tired, or flustered. The sentence tells us that after a shower and a change of clothes, she felt better, which suggests that the underlined word refers to her physical state. "Shredded" simply doesn't make sense. If a shower made her feel better, she probably didn't feel "beautiful" or "vivacious" (full of life and energy). This makes A, "unkempt," the best answer.

5. **C.** We talked about "florid" earlier: it means "flowery or embellished," lots of extra stuff that isn't necessary. Although something florid may be gorgeous, it isn't always. If you add to something, it's not in its natural state. Even if you didn't know what "inept" meant, you could make a pretty good educated guess that C, "embellished," is the best answer here.

Chapter 5

Paragraph Comprehension

In This Chapter

- Why you're tested on this
- Types of questions you'll see
- Techniques for choosing the best answer

Reading comprehension can be an intimidating section of any standardized test. You have to read through complicated and boring paragraphs on topics you may not have heard of and then answer questions based on what you read. It's really not as bad as it seems. In fact, a lot of times you can get away with reading only a few lines of the passage to get the correct answer. This chapter walks you through various types of Paragraph Comprehension questions, breaks down the passages into easy-to-handle parts, and shows you how to find the answers you want.

Why Do I Have to Take This?

As we said in Chapter 4, communication is a must-have skill in the military. Not only do you have to be able to effectively let others know what you're thinking, but you also have to be able to understand the way others are trying to communicate with you.

The Paragraph Comprehension (PC) section tests you on your reading and reasoning skills. The military wants to see if you have enough of a grasp of the English language to pay attention to details, draw conclusions, read between the lines, and follow instructions.

Basic Format

The basic format of a Paragraph Comprehension question is pretty, well, basic. You're given a short passage, which can be anywhere from a single paragraph to two or three. Then there can be a single question that follows or a few questions that all refer to one passage.

Most of us learned we should read the passage and then answer the question. But that doesn't make much sense on a timed test, especially with the ASVAB. You only have 13 minutes to answer 15 questions on the PAP version and 22 minutes to answer 11 questions on the CAT. If you only have to answer one question based on one paragraph, you could end up reading and trying to figure out a lot of information you'll never need to get your points—and wasting precious time.

We get into the best approach for each of the specific question types in a moment. For now, we want you to rethink your general approach to this type of test question:

1. **Read the question:** This tells you what type of question you're dealing with and what to look for in the passage. Also read through the answer choices and make sure you understand what they mean.

2. **Attack the passage:** Depending on what type of question you have, deploy the appropriate technique for best finding the information in the passage that will get you the answer you need. See "Types of Questions," later in the chapter.

3. **Answer and eliminate:** Following the four-step process from Chapter 3, answer the question in your own words and eliminate answer choices that don't match.

Test Tip

A correct answer in the Paragraph Comprehension section is always backed up directly with information from the passage. Reject answer choices that are not supported by a specific phrase or sentence in the passage.

Types of Questions

You'll usually see five types of questions on the ASVAB's Paragraph Comprehension subtest. Each is unique and has specific ways to find the right answer.

Main Idea

These questions ask you to figure out the overall point of the passage. Sometimes this is stated outright in the paragraphs, and sometimes you have to use the information given to figure it out.

Most passages have a predictable format. Some kind of topic sentence states or implies the point of the passage. The rest of the sentences give details or support to that point.

With main idea questions, you have to read the whole passage to figure out its purpose. The good thing about these questions is that there aren't as many of them as the other kinds.

Approach: Look for sentences that explain what the passage is about instead of how or why something is what it is. These can appear anywhere in the passage.

Tone

These questions ask you to identify what the speaker or narrator is feeling, based on the content of the passage. As with main idea questions, you have to read the whole passage for this one.

Approach: Look at the language being used, punctuation, and context clues to figure out whether the passage is portraying someone who is excited, somber, apprehensive, happy, and so on.

Try this example:

> Nothing in my closet is right for today, the most important of my life so far. How I look the first day of junior high school will determine how people see me through the next two years. I know, I'll wear the brown suede skirt. Wait. No, pants would make a better impression. Or maybe a dress.

What kind of vibe do you get from reading this paragraph? "Nervous," "unsure," and "cautious" are all good answers. The wavering of her decision indicates that's how she'd be feeling. The correct answer will have something to do with these emotions.

Specific Details

Some passages give you information about history, science, or art, or even take you through a process. When you see these types of passages, expect to find questions that ask you to find specific information close behind.

These are actually one of the easier types of questions you'll encounter, simply because the correct answer will most likely use the same language that's in the passage.

Approach: Determine what information the question is asking you to find, and then skim through the passage looking for key words or ideas that will most likely lead you to what you're looking for. Read the sentence that contains the information and then the sentences before and after, and you should have enough information to come up with the right answer.

Vocabulary-in-Context

As in the Word Knowledge section, you'll see questions in Paragraph Comprehension that ask you to define a word in context. Again, you're being tested not only on your vocabulary, but also on how that word is used in that specific sentence.

Approach: Since you're looking for specific information in this type of question, go back to the passage and read the sentence that contains the word in the question. Use context clues to determine how the word is being used and what it's intended to mean. Then eliminate answer choices that don't match your definition.

Inference

If you've ever read a novel, you may have noticed that the thrill of the story isn't so much in what the author writes on the page as it is what's not said, or *implied.*

Inference questions on the ASVAB ask you to draw logical conclusions about what someone associated with the passage might think, see, or do based on the information presented.

def•i•ni•tion

> To **imply** means that something suggests information without stating it outright. When you make the connection between what's said and what's implied, you infer. This type of question is called an **inference**; the passage implies something, and it's your job to infer what it might be.

These are the trickiest of the questions in this section because they ask you to come up with information that is not directly stated. However, correct answers will always be supported by specific details in the passage.

Approach: Read your question and answer choices first. Then read the passage. Go back to each answer choice and ask yourself, "What in the passage tells me this would likely happen or be true?"

Let's try this out:

> The author of this passage would most likely support
>
> (A) increased inclusion of organic foods in mainstream media.
>
> (B) a letter-writing campaign to lower the state speed limit.

(C) the opening of an independent natural foods store in a small town.

(D) a major grocery chain introducing a line of natural products that is less expensive than comparable name-brand items.

Now take a look at the passage:

> Organic foods and other natural products should be more accessible to the general consumer. Too often they are found only online, which requires shipping, or in specialty shops in remote areas. Being able to purchase a variety of organic foods at their local grocery store would make it easier for consumers to live healthy lifestyles and would also stimulate sales for this growing industry.

The author of this passage is clearly arguing for making organic and natural products more available for consumers to purchase. Compare this to the answer choices.

With answer choice A, consumers may become more aware of these products but will not be able to gain more access to them. Answer B implies some kind of government intervention, which is neither stated nor implied in the passage. Answer C is an example of a specialty shop in a remote area, which goes against the argument. That leaves us with answer D, which is an example of what is stated in the last sentence of the passage.

It's time to practice your technique.

Practice Questions

Read each paragraph and select the answer choice that best answers each question.

Use the following passage to answer questions 1–3:

Art therapy is a type of psychological engagement that employs nonverbal modes of expression to help uncover ideas and feelings, especially with children and in family counseling. Through drawing, painting, photography, and other types of artistic engagement, those engaging in art therapy produce works that can be interpreted by both the artist and counselor.

1. In the passage, the word <u>employs</u> most nearly means

   (A) to provide a job.

   (B) to anticipate.

   (C) to make use of.

   (D) to aggravate.

2. Based on the information in the passage, a likely candidate for art therapy would be

   (A) a convicted felon in prison.

   (B) a child who was involved in a car accident.

   (C) an adult who just lost her job.

   (D) a high school guidance counselor dealing with a troubled student.

3. The tone of the passage can be best
   described as

   (A) argumentative.

   (B) informal.

   (C) appreciative.

   (D) informative.

Use the following passage to answer questions 4
and 5:

> Recessions seem to be a natural part of
> the economic cycle and, therefore, can be
> predicted. Predicting factors include major
> drops in stock market indexes, significant
> rises in unemployment rates from quarter
> to quarter, and inverted yield curves, which
> happen when long-term investment yields
> are less than short-term yields. While these
> indicators do not guarantee a recession will
> happen, economists should still keep an eye
> out when any of these conditions arise.

4. The main idea of this passage is best
   described as

   (A) economists should look for signs of
   recessions.

   (B) recessions are inevitable.

   (C) a stock market crash indicates that a
   recession is near.

   (D) people should not invest during a
   recession.

5. According to the passage, each of the following is a predictor of a recession except

(A) a significant drop in the stock market.

(B) increased unemployment rates for at least six months.

(C) consecutive drops in the Gross Domestic Product.

(D) an inverted yield curve.

Answers and Explanations

1. **C.** "Employ" has several definitions, one of which is answer A. However, the sentence found in the passage does not refer to providing a job. "Anticipate" and "aggravate" don't make sense if you swap out "employ" for them in the sentence. Therefore, "to make use of" is the best answer.

2. **B.** The passage indicates that art therapy is used with children and those who need a way to communicate other than using words. Your ideal answer choice will have someone like this in the description, which eliminates answers A and C. Children are involved in the remaining choices, but answer D names the counselor as the candidate for art therapy, not the child. This makes B the best choice.

3. **D.** Overall, the passage is neutral, so you'll want to look for an answer choice that

reflects this. Answers A and C are negative and positive, respectively. The language used in the passage is more formal than conversational, and its purpose is clearly to inform. "Informative" is the best choice.

4. **A.** This is one of those cases in which the main idea comes in the last sentence of the passage. The transition "While these indicators do not guarantee a recession will happen" is a clue that the main idea is about to follow. Answers B and C really talk about why economists should try to look for signs of a recession, while answer D was not mentioned in the passage at all.

5. **C.** Here is one of those tricky detail questions that asks you to find the answer choice that's *not* mentioned in the passage. If you compare each choice to the predictors listed in the passage, you'll find that answer choice C is your best bet.

Practice is really the key to improving your PC score. Try to get as comfortable as you can with the types of reading you'll have to do, different ways of approaching the questions, and the time frame in which you'll have to complete this section *before* sitting down to take the exam.

Chapter 6

Word Problems Made Reasonable

In This Chapter

- Why the military tests you on this
- Types of questions to expect
- Strategies for success
- Essential arithmetic review

Of the two math sections on the ASVAB, Arithmetic Reasoning (AR) is by far the most practical. How so? It applies most of the math skills you've acquired throughout your life to real situations, giving you a good idea of why you needed to learn all that stuff in the first place.

Still, many people balk at the thought of tackling word problems—and with good reason. Very often (especially on standardized tests) they are worded funnily and are complicated or confusing. The ASVAB is no exception.

This chapter walks you through ways to make these reasoning problems more, well, reasonable. We show you how to break these questions into bite-size pieces that are easier to understand, in addition to giving you a review of basic concepts you'll likely encounter on the test.

Why Do I Have to Take This?

All branches of the military want to make sure their recruits can follow instructions carefully and logically. This is why Arithmetic Reasoning is required for the AFQT. It doesn't test your math skills as much as it does your ability to work through and solve problems.

What to Expect

The entire Arithmetic Reasoning section is made up of word problems that ask you to apply logic and simple arithmetic skills. Here's your first example of the type of question you can expect to see on this test:

> On the CAT version of the Arithmetic Reasoning subtest, you'll have 39 minutes to answer 16 questions. On the PAP, you'll have 36 minutes to answer 30 questions. How much more time per question do you have on the CAT versus the PAP?

As you can see, the questions in this section test your ability to break down a complex task into its individual parts and determine which mathematical operations you need to use to get the right answer.

Best Approach

Approaching a word problem is a lot like planning an attack on an enemy target. You have to gather intel on the target, assess the situation, devise a plan of attack, execute the mission, and debrief. You can use the same strategies with the Arithmetic Reasoning subtest, but tweaked for taking a test rather than doing battle:

1. **Gather intel:** In the field, you'd send someone on a reconnaissance mission to get information about a target. On the ASVAB, you simply read the question from beginning to end and try to figure out what it's asking you to do.

2. **Assess the situation:** After you've read the question, translate it into words that make sense to you. This will give you a better understanding of what the question is asking you to do, and give you a simpler version to work off when moving forward.

3. **Devise a plan of attack:** Write out the steps and equations you'll need to solve the problem. Seeing them on your scratch paper will help you keep track of your work as you go along and make sure you're taking a logical approach to solving the problem.

4. **Execute the mission:** Complete all steps needed to formulate the answer. Check and double-check your math to make sure that it's accurate and it makes sense.

5. **Debrief:** In real life, this is when you would report the results of your mission. On the ASVAB, this is when you eliminate answer choices that don't match the one you've come up with.

Let's try this approach on the word problem from the previous section:

1. On the CAT version of the Arithmetic Reasoning subtest, you'll have 39 minutes to answer 16 questions. On the PAP, you'll have 36 minutes to answer 30 questions. How much more time per question do you have on the CAT versus the PAP?

2. The question is asking us to find the difference (red flag for subtraction) between two times. But to get those times, we have to figure out how much time there is to answer each question (red flag for division) in each section.

3. We can set up three expressions to help us work through the problem: one to figure out how long you have to work on these questions on the CAT, one to do the same for the PAP, and one to calculate the difference. What you write on your scratch paper may look something like this:

Minutes per CAT question = $\dfrac{39}{16}$

Minutes per PAP question = $\dfrac{36}{30}$

Minutes per CAT question – minutes per PAP question = final answer

4. Now let's solve the expressions we've written and find out what answer choice we need to look for:

   $CAT = \dfrac{39}{16} = 39 \div 16 = 2.4375$ (minutes per CAT question)

   $PAP = \dfrac{36}{30} = 36 \div 30 = 1.2$ (minutes per PAP question)

   $CAT - PAP = 2.4375 - 1.2 = 1.2375$

5. If this were a question on the ASVAB, you'd now eliminate answer choices that are not in the ballpark of 1.2375 minutes. Instead, you can just hope to take the CAT version of the test because you get double the time to work on word problems than you do on the PAP.

Congrats! You've just painlessly solved your first ASVAB-style word problem. You can use this method on any word problem you encounter on the test and increase your chances of getting the correct answer. (If you're totally lost on how the previous equations were solved, skip forward to Chapter 7, which explains basic algebra and how to solve equations.)

Arithmetic Review

Let's start with some basic terms and symbols. Some may be familiar, while others may be new.

Arithmetic Vocab

Term	Definition
Natural numbers	Counting numbers, like 1, 2, 3, etc. Natural numbers are always positive, and 0 is not a natural number. When a set of natural numbers includes 0 (0, 1, 2, 3), you're dealing with whole numbers.
Integer	Any whole number and its opposite (the opposite of 3 is –3; the opposite of 5 is –5). –2, –1, 0, 1, and 2 are all integers; –3.1 and 2.5 are not.
Prime number	An integer that can only be divided by 1 and itself. 2, 3, 5, 7, 11, 13, and 17 are prime numbers. 1 is not a prime number because 1 is its only factor.
Factor	A number that can be evenly divided into a number. Factors of 12 are 1, 2, 3, 4, 6, and 12. They all divide into 12 evenly.
Multiple	The product of two natural numbers: 36 is a multiple of 9 since 9×4 is 36; 14 is a multiple of 7 since 7×2 is 14.
Product	Answer to a multiplication problem. This and words like "times," "double," and "of" in a word problem can indicate the need for multiplication.
Quotient	Answer to a division problem. This and words like "per," "out of," and "into" in a word problem can indicate the need for division.

Sum   Answer to an addition problem. This
                       and words like "total" and "com-
                       bined" in a word problem can
                       indicate the need for addition.

Difference   Answer to a subtraction problem.
                       This and words like "minus,"
                       "decrease," and "fall" in a word
                       problem can indicate the need for
                       subtraction.

Now you're ready to dive into subjects that are
often seen on the Arithmetic Reasoning subtest.

Order of Operations

In school, you may have learned about order of
operations, which applies when you have an expression with more than one type of operation symbol
(+, ×, ÷, and –). You need to follow a specific order
to solve these problems correctly.

Heads-Up

When you see a number or expression in parentheses, but no operation
directly before or after, you should multiply.

First, look for any expressions that are separated
into parentheses and solve these first with applying
any exponents (see Chapter 7) that may be present.
Next, move on to multiplication and division and
solve these parts of the expression moving left to

right. Finally, perform the addition and subtraction operations, moving left to right. Once the expression in the parentheses has been reduced to a number, repeat the order of operations on the entire expression. An easy way to remember this is with the mnemonic PE(MD)(AS) or "Please Excuse My Dear Aunt Sally."

Try this with the following expression:
$3 + 2 [1 + 2(1 + 2)]^2$

Start with the inner expression in parentheses and find 3 to be the answer (the brackets are there to indicate that when we're done with the operations within, the value that's left will be multiplied). The parentheses around the 3 indicate we must multiply. Within the brackets, we multiply 2×3 first, then add $1 + 6$. Next, apply the exponent to the 7 to get 49. Next, multiply 2×49 to get 98, and finally, add the 3. Your work should look like this:

$3 + 2 [1 + 2(3)]^2$

$3 + 2 [1 + 6]^2$

$3 + 2 [7]^2$

$3 + 2 \times 49$

$3 + 98$

101

Positive and Negative Integers

If you think of numbers in terms of a line, you'll be able to understand positives and negatives. At the center of the line is 0. All numbers to the right of 0 are positive, and all numbers to the left are negative.

Easy enough, right? The tricky part with positives and negatives comes when you start moving up and down that line through addition and subtraction. The number on the right of an expression tells you how many units to move and in which direction on the line. When you see an addition sign (+), you move to the right on the number line. When you see a subtraction sign (–), you move to the left.

Look at the following expression: 4 – 2. Your first instinct might be to read this as 4 minus 2, but really, what you're seeing in terms of the number line is +4 + (–2). This expression is telling you to start at the +4 position on the number line and move two steps to the left, or –2. The result is that you end up at +2 on the number line.

This is the basic idea how we deal with adding and subtracting positives and negatives in math. Use the number line above to illustrate the following:

- Positive + positive = Move up the number line: 2 + 2 = 4

- Positive + negative = Move down the number line: $2 + (-3) = -1$
- Negative + positive = Move up the number line: $-4 + 6 = 2$
- Negative + negative = Move down the number line: $-2 + (-2) = -4$
- Negative – negative = When you have two negative symbols, they cancel each other out and make a positive. For example, $-3 - (-4)$ is the same as $-3 + 4$, and you would move up the number line when you solve. The answer is $+1$.
- Positive – negative = With this type of problem, you have a negative as well: $1 - (-2)$. The negative becomes a positive, and so you need to move up the number line: $1 + 2 = 3$.

Multiplication and division problems are a little different. First, you should multiply or divide the numbers in the problem as you normally would. After you get your answer, you need to figure out whether it's positive or negative. Only the negatives affect the sign of the answer:

- An odd number of negatives will result in a *negative* answer: $-14 \div 7 = -2$ (one negative); $(-2)(-4)(-5) = -40$ (three negatives).
- An even number of negatives will result in a *positive* answer: $-27 \div -3 = 9$ (two negatives); $(-4)(-6)(-8)(-10) = 1920$ (four negatives).

Multiples and Factors

Here, we're going to talk about how numbers are made up of other numbers in terms of factors (the product of two natural numbers).

Think about the number 4. How many ways can you calculate this number through multiplication? Just two: 1×4 and 2×2. Guess what? You just calculated the factors of 4! 1, 2, and 4 are all factors of 4.

You should know three main things when calculating with multiples and factors:

- **Prime factorization:** This action breaks down a number into the product of its prime factors, which can make finding a Greatest Common Factor or Least Common Multiple (both of which have been known to pop up on the ASVAB) much quicker.

   Start with the number you're trying to factor out and then divide it by a prime number. Do this again and again until you have 1 as an answer. Then list all of the primes you used and multiply. Let's try this with the number 20:

   $2\underline{|20}$
   $2\underline{|10}$
   $5\underline{|5}$
   1

Now list out the prime numbers you've used on the outside (2, 2, and 5) and then multiply: $2 \times 2 \times 5 = 20$. You've just calculated the prime factors of 20.

- **Greatest common factor (GCF):** The general idea here is to multiply all the common prime factors of two numbers. The product is the highest factor they have in common.

To find the GCF of two numbers, use prime factorization and multiply the common factors. Then calculate any exponent and multiply the shared factors.

Now it's your turn. Find the greatest common factor of 28 and 36:

```
     2|36
2|28  2|18
2|14  3|9
7|7   3|3
1     1
```

$28 = 2 \times 2 \times 7$

$36 = 2 \times 2 \times 3 \times 3$

The only shared factor here is 2×2, or 2^2, which, when multiplied, gives you a highest common factor of 4. If there had been more than one shared factor, you would multiply them all, and the product would be your greatest common factor.

- **Least common multiple (LCM):** Use prime factorization to figure out the smallest number that can be divided by two specific numbers. Reduce each number down to its prime factors. Then multiply each factor by the greatest number of times it appears in any one factorization. Take a look at the following example, where you need to find the LCM of 10 and 24:

$10 = 2 \times 5$

$24 = 2 \times 2 \times 2 \times 3$

$2 \times 2 \times 2 \times 3 \times 5 = 120$

As you can see, the greatest number of times we see 2 is three, 3 is one, and 5 is one. We then combined each of these occurrences in the equation $2 \times 2 \times 2 \times 3 \times 5 =$ and found that 120 is the smallest number that 10 and 24 can both divide into evenly.

Fractions

Fractions represent a part of a whole, which means that every number can be expressed as a fraction. They follow a specific format: $\frac{4}{8}$. The bottom number (denominator) tells us how many pieces make up the whole. The top number (numerator) tells us how many parts of that whole we are dealing with.

A few things to remember:

- When the numerator is less than the denominator, you have a proper fraction: $\frac{1}{4}$

- When the numerator and denominator are the same number, the fraction equals 1:
$$\frac{4}{4} = 1$$

- When the numerator is either equal to or greater than the denominator, you have an improper fraction, which represents something that is either more than or equal to 1:
$$\frac{9}{4}$$

- When you simplify an improper fraction, you break it down into a mixed fraction, which includes a whole number. Divide the bottom number into the top (that result is your whole number) and use the remainder as the numerator of a new fraction with the denominator remaining the same: $\frac{9}{4} = 2\frac{1}{4}$.

The main things you should know about working with proper fractions on the ASVAB are:

- **Simplifying:** This reduces a fraction to its simplest form. Break down both the numerator and denominator into prime factors and get rid of any factors each side has in common. What's left is the simplified fraction:
$$\frac{9}{27} = \frac{3 \times 3}{3 \times 3 \times 3} = \frac{\cancel{3} \times \cancel{3}}{\cancel{3} \times \cancel{3} \times 3} = \frac{1}{3}$$

  You should always reduce your fractions before attempting any other action with them.

- **Adding:** When you add proper fractions, you add only the numerators, once your denominators are the same. If you find yourself with two fractions that have different denominators, don't panic: a quick and easy way to make your denominators match is to multiply each fraction by the opposite denominator as both numerator and denominator.

For example, if you wanted to add $\frac{4}{5} + \frac{2}{4}$,

you would multiply the first fraction by $\frac{4}{4}$,

since the opposite denominator is 4. You would multiply the second fraction by $\frac{5}{5}$,

since 5 is the denominator opposite the 4 in the second fraction. The result is:

$\frac{4}{5} \times \frac{4}{4} = \frac{16}{20}$ and $\frac{2}{4} \times \frac{5}{5} = \frac{10}{20}$.

Now add the numerators on the resulting fractions and find that:

$\frac{16}{20} + \frac{10}{20} = \frac{26}{20}$

An improper fraction, like the one in the previous example, has a larger numerator over a smaller denominator. This means that the fraction is more than a whole. Simplify this by dividing the top number by the bottom one and making the remainder the top number of the new fraction. Then reduce:

$26 \div 20 = 1\frac{6}{20} = 1\frac{3}{10}$

- **Subtracting:** The same rules you would apply for addition, you use for subtraction:

$$\frac{4}{5} - \frac{2}{4} = \frac{16}{20} - \frac{10}{20} = \frac{6}{20} = \frac{3}{10}$$

- **Multiplying:** Multiplying fractions is pretty straightforward. Just multiply the numerators and denominators straight across, and then simplify the resulting fraction:

$$\frac{5}{8} \times \frac{6}{7} = \frac{30}{56} = \frac{15}{28}$$

- **Dividing:** Dividing fractions doesn't really involve division. When you have to divide two fractions, set up your problem as if you were multiplying. Then flip the numbers of the second fraction and multiply across:

$$\frac{5}{8} \div \frac{6}{7} = \frac{5}{8} \times \frac{7}{6} = \frac{35}{48}$$

Decimals

These, too, represent portions of a whole, but in a different way than fractions. Instead of using a line to represent parts of a whole number, we use a decimal point.

Just as every whole number is a fraction, every whole number is a decimal. The decimal place is directly behind the whole number: 4 = 4.0. Keeping the decimal in the right place is the trick when you're dealing with the various ways you may see decimal questions on the ASVAB.

Important things to remember:

Adding and subtracting: Stack your expressions so that the decimal points line up before you attempt to solve these problems. This ensures that you keep your numbers in line and that your answer has the decimal in the right place.

Multiplying: It's easiest to ignore the decimal points when multiplying decimals. Simply multiply the problem as you normally would. Then count up the *total* number of decimal places in *each* factor of the original expression, and put the decimal point that many places to the left of the last number in your product.

Take a look at this example: $12.65 \times 5.2 = 1265 \times 52 = 65780$. There are three decimal places in the original expression (two numbers after the decimal in the first factor and one number after the decimal in the second factor), so we need to put the decimal point three places to the left of the 0. The answer is 65.780 or 65.78. You can drop any zeroes at the end whenever you deal with decimals.

Dividing: Dividing decimals is pretty easy. Say you have to solve the following problem: $463.55 \div 2.347$. When you write this out on your scratch paper, it will probably look like this: $2.3\overline{)463.55}$. Here, you want to move the decimal point in 2.347 three places to the right so that you have a whole number: 2347.

Next, you need to move the decimal the same number of spaces in your dividend: 463.55. But you only have two decimal places to work with, so what do you do? Whenever you're dividing decimals, you can add as many zeroes to the end of the dividend as you need to in order to complete the equation. In this case, you would add a 0 to the end of the dividend and then move the decimal three places to the right, making the whole number 463550.

Your new equation is $2347\overline{)463550}$, which has the decimal point after the 0. Simply divide 2347 into 463550 and move the decimal point straight up. Your answer should be 197.5.

Decimals to fractions: You should also know how to convert a fraction to a decimal, and vice versa. If you divide the numerator by the denominator, the answer is a decimal.

To convert a decimal to a fraction, make the decimal the numerator and 1 the denominator. Then move the decimal point to the right until you have a whole number. For each place you move the decimal to the right, add a zero to the denominator. Finally, simplify the fraction: $.25 = \dfrac{.25}{1} = \dfrac{25}{100} = \dfrac{1}{4}$

Percent

Percents are another way to express a portion of a whole, but on a fixed scale. Whenever you have a question that involves percent, you're dealing with either decimals or fractions (whichever works best for you). The difference is that percents represent a part of 100.

In decimals, 100 percent is the same as 1. Anything less than 100 percent is shown to the right of the decimal place: 4% = .04; 50% = .50.

In fractions, 100 percent is $\frac{100}{100}$. When you want to turn a whole number into a percent expressed as a fraction, simply make the number the numerator and use 100 as the denominator: $4\% = \frac{4}{100}$. Then, if possible, reduce.

In the AR section of the ASVAB, having to calculate percentages of a value is a common task. When asked to do this, convert the percentage to a decimal or fraction and then multiply it by the value because "of" indicates multiplication. If you're asked to calculate an increase or decrease in percentage, do the same thing and either add or subtract from the original value stated. Try it here:

> The base commissary has increased the price of greeting cards by 15%. You bought a card there last year for $2.25. How much can you expect to pay for the same card today?

This question is asking you to figure out how much a 15% increase will raise the price of a card. You need to do two things to solve this. First, figure out how much 15% of $2.25 is in dollars. This works out to be about $.34 (.15 × 2.25 = .3375). Now add $2.25 + .34, and you'll get your final answer of $2.59.

Ratios

Ratios are expressed in three main ways: with fractions, with a colon (:), or using the word *to*. However you say it, a ratio is a mathematical way to compare two values. Ratios on the ASVAB usually express some sort of group relationship:

> You pull a handful of change out of your pocket. As you count the coins, you realize you have 10 dimes and 15 pennies. What is the ratio of dimes to pennies in your pocket?

To work this out, start by making this into a fraction: $\frac{10}{15}$. This shows the relationship between the two types of coins and is the same as saying that the ratio of dimes to pennies is 10 to 15, or 10:15. As with a fraction, you should simplify this down to read $\frac{2}{3}$. Remember that the way you read it is the way you write it.

Proportions

Proportions are a comparison of ratios. It's easiest to treat these as fractions as well. You can do a couple things with proportions. The first is to test whether they are equal. To do this, you cross-multiply the fractions. If the products are the same, your proportions are equal.

Try this example: $\frac{9}{18} = \frac{1}{2}$. To find out if these proportions are equal, multiply 9×2 and 18×1. The products are both 18, so they are equal.

The other thing you can do with proportions is solve for an unknown quantity. You'll likely see or set up two fractions joined with an equals sign. This time, however, there will be a variable, which is a letter that stands in for the value we're looking to find:

$$\frac{4}{6} = \frac{x}{15}$$
$$15 \times 4 = 60$$
$$6 \times x = 60$$

To find the value of x, divide both sides by 6. This gives you a final answer of $x = 10$.

Test Tip

For questions like these, you can also substitute the answer choices for the unknown value. This can save you some time and effort.

Probability

This area of math calculates the chances of something happening. Questions on the ASVAB that deal with probability will likely have either "probability" or "chance of" somewhere in the problem.

You'll also probably have several steps to take to calculate the answer:

> The flight school you want to get into accepts only 15 recruits per quarter. Six recruits have already been accepted, and 20 others (yourself included) have applied. What is the probability that you will land a spot in the school?

To figure out a probability, use the following formula: $P = \dfrac{\text{Number of possibilities}}{\text{Number of possible outcomes}}$.

The number of possible outcomes is 15 because only 15 recruits will be accepted. If 6 have already been accepted, this lowers the total possible spots to 9. Since there are 20 people who could possibly be chosen, the probability you will be one is $\dfrac{9}{20}$.

It's time try out some of this stuff for real.

Heads-Up

A correct probability will always be a value between 0 and 1. If you come up with an improper fraction, you know there's an error somewhere in your work.

Practice Questions

Break down each of the following questions and choose the best answer out of what's given. Don't forget that you can't use a calculator on the test, so make sure you have a pencil and paper nearby to help you figure out these problems.

1. A class of 126 students fills out surveys about their future plans. Every student responds: 36 women and 90 men. If $\frac{3}{4}$ of the women and $\frac{5}{6}$ of the male respondents said they were going to college, how many total students said they are pursuing other options?

   (A) 15

   (B) 22

   (C) 24

   (D) 102

2. A dance club starts letting people in at 9:00 P.M. In the first hour, 25 men and 35 women are admitted, and none leave. In the second hour, 32 men and 48 women are admitted. Again none leave. In the third hour, 8 women and 7 men leave, and no more people are admitted into the club. What is the ratio of men to women in the club by midnight?

   (A) 2:3

   (B) 5:6

   (C) 8:3

   (D) 10:1

3. If a car costs $2,567, how much money would you owe if you made a down payment of one-third of the price?

    (A) $19.95

    (B) $855.67

    (C) $1,711.33

    (D) $2,211.25

4. A bag holds four red beads, five blue beads, and nine black beads. If you reach into the bag, what is the probability you will draw a blue bead?

    (A) $\dfrac{5}{9}$

    (B) $\dfrac{9}{18}$

    (C) $\dfrac{3}{9}$

    (D) $\dfrac{5}{18}$

Answers and Explanations

1. **C.** This one is tricky. First, you need to figure out how many men and women answered that they plan to go college:

$$\frac{3}{4} \times \frac{36}{1} = \frac{108}{4} = 27 \text{ women}$$

$$\frac{5}{6} \times \frac{90}{1} = \frac{450}{6} = 75 \text{ men}$$

Then add these two totals together to find that 102 students plan to go to college. Don't stop there, though. You need to find how many students *don't* plan to go to college. Subtract 102 from the total number of students, and you have answer C.

2. **A.** Add the number of men and women who have come into the club throughout the night. Keep your totals separate. Then subtract the number of patrons who left in the third hour, and you have 50 men and 75 women. Calculate the ratio by reducing $\frac{50}{75}$ to $\frac{2}{3}$. Your answer is A, 2:3.

3. **C.** Calculate how much one third of $2,567 is: $\frac{1}{3} \times \frac{2567}{1} = \frac{2567}{3} = 2567 \div 3 = 855.67$. Subtract that amount from the total cost, and your answer is C.

4. **D.** There are 18 beads total. Of those, only 5 are blue, leaving you only 5 chances out of 18 to draw a blue bead: $\frac{5}{18}$.

While many of the concepts discussed in the chapter may be review to you, it's a good idea to practice these skills before taking the test. The best way to brush up is repetition, especially with word problems. The more you work through them, the easier they become.

Chapter 7

Re-Up Your Math Knowledge

In This Chapter

- Why the military tests you on this
- Types of questions to expect
- Strategies for success
- Essential review for each subject area

"When am I ever going to use this in real life?" This has been the question most often asked of math teachers everywhere. One of the answers is simply that you'll need to know it to pass standardized tests throughout your life, including the ASVAB. The good news is that the ASVAB tests you only on the basics of what you've learned throughout grammar school and high school. There's no trig or calculus here, but you can expect some algebra and geometry.

This chapter gives you a quick review of the different areas that have been known to pop up on the Mathematics Knowledge (MK) section of the

ASVAB, as well as techniques for approaching these problems.

Why Do I Have to Take This?

Unlike many of your high school math classes, the Mathematics Knowledge section of the ASVAB will test you on more practical applications that you need to know to perform just about any job in the military. This could explain why it's part of the AFQT, which you need to pass in order to gain entrance to the military as a whole. It's also required for many MOS positions. Either way, it's a necessity.

What to Expect

Mathematics Knowledge is a relatively short section. On the CAT, you need to answer 16 questions in 20 minutes (1.25 minutes per question). For the PAP, you've got 25 questions in 24 minutes (just under a minute each). It's a good idea to know which version you're taking (see Chapter 2) when you prep for this section so that you can budget your time wisely and play to your strengths.

Expect straightforward equations, questions about math concepts, and short word problems. Many questions will have several steps that need to be taken in order to come up with the correct answer, so be prepared to look beyond the surface before attacking any of these questions.

Test Tip

You're not allowed to bring a calculator into the exam room, so make the most of the scratch paper you're given.

Strategic Attack

Before we get into the ins and outs of algebra and geometry, let's talk strategy. Math sections of standardized tests tend to trip people up because they're looking for traps and such. But we have a few tricks up our sleeve that help take some of the guesswork out of working on this section of the ASVAB:

- **Translate:** Standardized tests are notorious for asking you to complete complex questions with many steps. Take some time to really read the question before diving in. You may find that it's asking you to do something other than what you thought at first glance.

- **Estimate:** After reading the question, see if you can estimate what you're looking for in an answer. For example, if you know the answer to the question is going to be less than 100, eliminate everything that's 100 or more. This is a quick way to narrow your choices and help you decide if the answer you've calculated is reasonable.

- **Substitute:** If the question you're dealing with asks you to solve for a variable, try to plug the answer choices into the equation you're working with. This means you don't have to deal with unknowns and you can do simple math with real numbers. The right answer is the one that works in the equation.

- **Eliminate:** Again, we can't stress enough how important it is to eliminate answer choices you know are wrong.

As you go through our practice questions or test yourself with sample exams, try these techniques and see which work best for you.

Algebra Review

It may sound strange, but math is a language unto itself. It has sentences and expressions, just like English! So before we dive into the basic concepts of algebra, familiarize yourself with the terms in the following table.

Algebra Vocab

Term	Definition
Expression	Mathematical statement that combines terms and operations, such as $2 + 4$, $4x(14)$, or $3x^2 + 4x - 2$.
Operation	Action you need to take with a value: addition, subtraction, division, and multiplication.
Equation	A mathematical statement that shows two equal expressions: $14 + 22 = 36$ or $2x = 4$.

Variable	Letter in an equation or expression that stands in place of an unknown quantity; in $2x = 4$, x is the variable.
Coefficient	Number that multiplies a variable; in $2x = 4$, 2 is the coefficient and means $2 \times x$.
Term	A single number, variable, or combinations thereof. Examples: $10x$, xy^5, x, 20.
Constant	A number that stands by itself in an expression or equation; in $3x + 5$, 5 is the constant.

Now let's look at some initial concepts that will help you on a number of ASVAB questions.

Equations

Solving algebraic equations is a balancing act. Because there is an equals sign, it's your job to make sure that what's being expressed on both sides stays equal.

When you're looking to solve an equation, your goal is to determine the value of a variable. This is easier than you may think. The best way to do this is to get rid of everything you can on one side of the equation until all you're left with is your unknown variable.

How do you do this while keeping both sides balanced? Follow one simple rule, and you'll be in good shape: don't do anything to one side that you can't do to the other. Check out this example: $-9 + x = -2$.

You want to isolate the x in this equation to be the only thing to the left of the equals sign. To do this, you need to cancel out the –9 by adding 9 to both sides:

$$-9 + x = -2$$
$$9 - 9 + x = -2 + 9$$

The nines cancel each other out, so now you're left with only x on that side: $x = -2 + 9$.

The rest is simple arithmetic. If you remember from Chapter 6, when you add a positive to a negative, you actually end up subtracting the negative value from the positive one. In this case, $9 - 2 = 7$, which leaves you with a final answer of $x = 7$.

Exponents and Roots

Exponents can seem scary, but they really aren't once you learn a little about them. The main number in the term is called the *base*, while the raised number is the *exponent*. When you see this construction together, you have a power. For example, in 3^2, 3 is the base, ^{2} is the exponent, and all together it's called 3 to the second power (or 3 squared).

When you see a power, the exponent simply tells you to multiply the base times itself a certain number of times. If you translate the previous example, it's really 3×3.

Sometimes you'll see a negative exponent, such as 3^{-2}. When you see a negative exponent like this one, it's not telling you the number of times a number to multiply the base number by itself, but instead how many times to divide it. The easiest way to do that is to calculate the value of the exponent without the negative, then write the answer as a reciprocal fraction (see Chapter 6). Take a look at how this works with 3^{-2}. First, calculate the value of 3^2: $3 \times 3 = 9$. Then, write the answer as a reciprocal fraction. Since the number 9 is the same as $\frac{9}{1}$, you would simply flip that fraction. The final answer is $3^{-2} = \frac{1}{9}$.

Heads-Up

An exponent to the first power (x^1) is just the base shown. An exponent to the zero power (x^0) equals 1.

Some rules to remember with exponents:

- When you multiply like variables, you get an exponent: $y \times y = y^2$.
- When multiplying two like variables with exponents, keep the variable the same and add the exponents: $x^2 + x^4 = x^6$.
- When you apply an exponent to terms in parentheses that have powers, you multiply exponents to simplify the expression: $(x^3)^3 = x^{3 \times 3} = x^9$.

- When you multiply separate powers, you multiply the coefficients and then add the exponents: $x^2 \times x^2 \times x^2 = x^9$.
- When you multiply unlike variables with exponents, combine them into one term: $x^2 \times y^2 = x^2 y^2$.

A number or variable that is raised to the second power is called a *square*. The opposite of a squared base is a square root, the number that, when multiplied by itself, equals that power. For example, $8^2 = 8 \times 8 = 64$. If you wanted to find the square root of 64, your expression would be $\sqrt{64} = 8$.

For the ASVAB, it's easier to learn some common square roots than to learn how to break them down. Exponents from 1 to 10 are pretty easy: $\sqrt{4} = 2$, $\sqrt{9} = 3$, $\sqrt{16} = 4$, and so on. But what if you get a problem that looks like this:

1. $\sqrt{196}$

    (A) 12
    (B) 13
    (C) 14
    (D) 15

Knowing the squares of the first 20 natural numbers can help you quickly zero in on the correct square root answer. Make a list of squares from 1 to 20, and memorize them to maximize your knowledge. Here are some to start with: $2 \times 2 = 4$, $3 \times 3 = 9$, $4 \times 4 = 16$, and $5 \times 5 = 25$.

Polynomials

Okay, it's a big word, but all it really means is that you're looking at an expression with one or more terms that may be separated by an operation. You should be aware of four basic types of polynomials.

- **Monomial:** This is a polynomial that has just one term: 7, $14x$, and $2xy^4$ are all monomials.

- **Binomial:** This is an expression with two terms joined by operations: $6y + 4x$ and $2 - 9$ are binomials.

- **Trinomial:** This is an expression with three terms joined by operations: $x^2 + 4y - 2$ is a trinomial.

- **Polynomial:** This is any expression that has more than three terms.

On the ASVAB, you'll be asked to add, subtract, multiply, and divide much more complicated polynomial expressions and equations than the ones you've seen so far. A few rules to remember when you're dealing with polynomials:

- **Simplify before you solve:** Combine like terms (terms that have the same variables and exponent). To do this, simply add the coefficients. For example, with $2x^2 + 14x + x - xy = $, you can add $14x$ and x to make $15x$ because they share the exact same variable and exponent.

- **Multiply or divide:** Where you can, apply multiplication and/or division operations. To do this, multiply or divide coefficients as you normally would. Then move on to the variables and exponents. For example, with $(12x)$ $(4x^2y)$, multiply 12×4 and $x \times x \times x \times y$, to come up with $48x^3y$. With division, treat the operation like a fraction. For example, with $\dfrac{15x^5}{35x^3}$, you would reduce the coefficients as you would any fraction: $\dfrac{3x^5}{7x^3}$. Next, reduce the exponents. An easy way to do that is to write out the base the number of times indicated in the exponent : $\dfrac{\cancel{x} \times \cancel{x} \times \cancel{x} \times x \times x}{\cancel{x} \times \cancel{x} \times \cancel{x}}$. In this example, the bottom three x's cancel out three of the x's on the top, leaving two behind. Your final answer to this problem would be $\dfrac{3x^2}{7x}$.

- **Use FOIL when multiplying or dividing binomials:** FOIL stands for "first, outer, inner, and last," or the order you would multiply or divide terms. To simplify $(x + 2)$ $(x + 4)$, you multiply *first* terms $x \times x$, *outer* terms $x \times 4$, *inner* terms $2 \times x$, and *last* terms 2×4.

  Then add them all together following the order of operations:

  $(x + 2)$ $(x + 4) = (x \times x) + (x \times 4) + (2 \times x) + (4 \times 2)$

  $(x + 2)$ $(x + 4) = (x^2) + (4x) + (2x) + (8)$

  $(x + 2)$ $(x + 4) = x^2 + 6x + 8$

Let's try it again with something a little more complex: $(2x + 2)(3x - 3)$.

Use FOIL:

$(2x + 2)(3x - 3) = (2x \times 3x) + (2x \times -3) + (2 \times 3x) + (2 \times -3)$

Now solve what's in parentheses using the order of operations:

$(2x + 2)(3x - 3) = (6x^2) + (-6x) + (6x) + (-6)$

Combine like terms:

$(2x + 2)(3x - 3) = 6x^2 + -6$

Factoring Polynomials

Factoring polynomials is a common algebraic task that challenges you to find out what smaller expressions make up a larger expression. This means you have to work backward to figure out what was multiplied to get the expression or equation you're given.

Let's start with simple factoring. The first thing you need to do is figure out the GCF (see Chapter 6), or the greatest factor that two or more terms share (variables included). If variables are also involved, you need to look for the variable term with the lowest common exponent. For example, if you're looking for the GCF for $28x^3 + 36x$, your GCF would actually be $4x$ because x^1 is shared by both terms.

Once you've determined the GCF, break down each term into prime factors and take out the GCF from each. Place the simplified terms separated by their operations in parentheses and place the GCF outside. Let's try it. Factor the following expression: $10y + 15xy + 50y^2$.

Common factors are 5 and y, which, when multiplied, equal $5y$. Now that you have a GCF, break down each term into prime factors:

$10y = 2 \times 5 \times y$

$15xy = 5 \times 3 \times x \times y$

$50y^2 = 5 \times 5 \times 2 \times y \times y$

Simplify each of these by crossing out one $5 \times y$ in each expression:

$10y = 2 \times \cancel{5 \times y}$

$15xy = 3 \times \cancel{5 \times} x \times y$

$50y^2 = 2 \times y \times \cancel{5 \times} 5 \times y$

Simplify each term and place the new expression in parentheses with 5y outside: $10y + 15xy + 50y^2 = 5y (2 + 3x + 10y)$.

Now that you have a good idea how to work simple factoring, let's move on to something a little more complicated: factoring quadratic expressions. This is a common ASVAB task, and you approach it differently.

If you're presented with an expression that has the following structure or if the expression you're left with after factoring out the GCF has this structure, think quadratic expression: $ax^2 + bx + c$. Here, the x's can be any variable, and a, b, and c are coefficients. All of the following are quadratic expressions:

$y^2 + 11y + 30$; $x^2 + 10x + 25$; $a^2 + 7a + 12$

When you factor quadratic expressions, you're actually working FOIL backward to find the two binomials that when multiplied make up the quadratic. You do this in a few simple steps, which we'll show you using $a^2 + 7a + 12$.

First, create two sets of binomials with the expression's variable as the first term: (a) (a).

To figure out the second terms in each of the parentheses, list out the factors of the last term. Now find one that when added together equals the coefficient of the middle term. With the previous example, we would break down 12 into factors: 1×12, 2×6, and 3×4. (It's a good idea to do this with negatives as well.)

When you add 3 and 4, you have 7, which is the coefficient of the middle term. Plug these numbers into the parentheses: (a + 3) (a + 4). Finally, figure out whether you need positive or negative signs and where. Because both 3 and 4 are positive, use an addition in both sets of parenthesis. If the 3, 4, or both had negatives, you would use a subtraction sign in the parentheses.

Test Tip

If you want to save a lot of time and brain power, when you're asked to factor a quadratic expression, FOIL the answer choices. The one that equals the expression in the question is your answer.

Geometry Review

Geometry deals with lines, angles, and shapes. On the ASVAB, you're asked to apply basic geometric principles to specific circumstances. But the type of geometry that's on the ASVAB concentrates mostly on a handful of concepts that, once you brush up on, will get you through. Familiarize yourself with the terminology in the following table.

Geometry Vocab

Term	Definition
Polygon	A closed two-dimensional shape made up of at least three sides. Examples are a triangle, a hexagon, and a quadrilateral.
Area	The space an object occupies. Usually measured in square units.
Perimeter	The distance around an object.
Vertex	The point where the two lines that make up an angle intersect.
Line	A 180-degree angle that stretches infinitely in two directions.
Line segment	Part of a line with two endpoints.
Ray	Part of a line that has one finite endpoint but goes on infinitely in one direction.

Lines

Lines form the basis of geometry, and you'll see them in many forms. The most important things to know about lines are that they're infinite (they stretch in either direction without end) and they can be segmented, for the purposes of an ASVAB question.

A line segment is a part of a line with two endpoints. It's often broken up into several smaller segments, which are labeled with letters. The midpoint is the marking directly in the center of the segment.

You may be asked to identify certain parts of a line segment, such as its midpoint; calculate the length of a line segment based on information given; or apply properties of certain types of lines to figure out lengths or angle values.

Parallel lines are a special type of line, which we discuss in more detail in the next section. These are two lines that run next to each other but never meet.

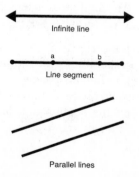

Infinite line

Line segment

Parallel lines

Angles

Angles are simply two rays that intersect at a common point and are measured in degrees. A straight line is a 180° angle. This is an important number to remember because it can help you calculate the degrees of other angles in a geometry question.

Some other common angles include these:

- **Right:** Angle that looks like an *L*. It measures 90°; the lines are perpendicular.
- **Adjacent:** Two angles that share a common side. It looks like it's split at the vertex. The sum of the two angles is equal to the larger angle.
- **Supplementary:** Two angles that together make a straight line. The sum of the angles equals 180°.
- **Complementary:** Two angles that make a right angle, so the sum of the angles equals 90°.
- **Acute:** Any angle that is less than 90°.
- **Obtuse:** Any angle that is more than 90°.
- **Corresponding:** You'll often see these as a set of parallel lines with another line running through both. This creates a set of angles with specific properties and relationships. Memorize the relationships outlined on the following diagram.

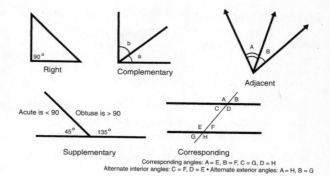

Right

Complementary

Adjacent

Acute is < 90   Obtuse is > 90

45°   135°

Supplementary

Corresponding

Corresponding angles: A = E, B = F, C = G, D = H
Alternate interior angles: C = F, D = E • Alternate exterior angles: A = H, B = G

Triangles

A lot of times, questions involving triangles and angles ask you to determine missing values before you get to the main part of the problem, which may be calculating area or some other task. Memorize these rules so you'll be able to get those missing values quickly:

- Triangles have three internal angles (see the diagram of an equilateral triangle later in this section). They also have external angles, which are adjacent.

- The three internal angles of a triangle always add up to 180°.

- The sum of an internal angle and its adjacent external angle always add up to 180°.

- You can calculate the value of an internal angle if you know the value of the adjacent external angle. Simply subtract the value of the external angle from 180.

- You can figure out the value of an external angle by adding the two internal angles that do not touch the external angle.

Special triangles have special rules:

- **Similar triangles:** Two triangles with equal internal angles, which makes the sides of each triangle proportional to the other.
- **Congruent triangles:** Two triangles that have the exact side lengths and angles.
- **Isosceles:** A triangle with two sides of equal length and two angles that are equal.
- **Equilateral:** A triangle with all side lengths and angles equal. Angles are always 60°.
- **Right:** A triangle with one angle equal to 90°.

Isosceles

Equilateral

Right

Three main calculations are associated with triangles:

- **Perimeter:** Add the values of all three sides using the equation $P = a + b + c$.
- **Area:** Determine the length of the base of a triangle, divide by half, and then multiply by the height using the equation $A = \frac{1}{2}bh$.

The base of a triangle is the length of the bottom line, and the height is the distance between the triangle's highest point and the base. Often you'll see this indicated as a dotted line running from the base to the top angle. A triangle's area is represented in square units (cm^2, ft^2) when units of measure are given in the problem.

● **Missing side of a right triangle:** When you know the value of any two sides of a right triangle, you can use the Pythagorean Theorem to calculate the other: $a^2 + b^2 = c^2$. Use this formula by substituting in the two sides that you know and algebraically solve for the missing side.

Pythagorean Theorem

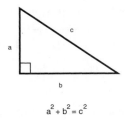

$$a^2 + b^2 = c^2$$

Quadrilaterals

These are polygons with four sides and corners. You should know these main types of quadrilaterals.

- **Parallelogram:** A quadrilateral in which opposite sides are equal in length and parallel, which makes opposite angles also equal. Rectangles, rhombi, and squares are all parallelograms.
- **Rectangles:** Parallelogram with four right angles. The sides that run parallel to each other are equal.
- **Squares:** All four sides are the same value and angles are right angles.

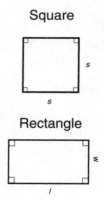

Perimeter calculations are the same as with triangles; simply add the values of the sides. If one of the values is missing, look to see if you can determine the value based on the properties of the quadrilateral. For example, if you have to find the perimeter of a square but know only one side, you multiply that value by 4. To calculate area, you multiply length and width values ($A = lw$).

Circles

Circles often seem like tricky creatures. Get to know them better, and you'll change your mind. Some essential bits of information:

- **Radius (*r*):** This is a line that's drawn from the center of a circle to the edge. A circle can have an infinite number of radii.
- **Diameter (*d*):** Double the value of any radius, and you get the length of the diameter.
- **Circumference (*c*):** This is the distance around a circle.
- **Chord:** This is a line in a circle that touches any two points of the edge.
- **pi (π):** This is a mathematical constant that appears in many formulas involving circles. All you need to know is that it equals about 3.14, which is enough to get you through your ASVAB calculations.

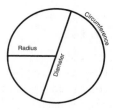

These gems of wisdom about circles and the following formulas should help you tackle just about any circle question on the ASVAB:

- Circumference: $c = 2\pi r$
- Area: $A = \pi r^2$

Practice Questions

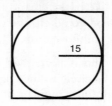

1. The difference between the area of the circle and the area of the square in the diagram above is
   (A) 193.5
   (B) 522.6
   (C) 709
   (D) 900

2. Factor $x^2 + 12x - 28 = 0$
   (A) $(y - 3)(x + 2)$
   (B) $(x + 7)(x - 4)$
   (C) $(x + 14)(x - 2)$
   (D) $(x - 14)(x - 2)$

3. Solve for x: $(12 - 3)^2 + (\frac{6}{3}) - (\sqrt{49}) = \frac{380}{x}$
   (A) 2
   (B) 5
   (C) 15
   (D) 60

4. Which of the following is NOT a prime number?

   (A) 2

   (B) 6

   (C) 7

   (D) 13

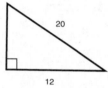

5. The area of the above triangle is most nearly

   (A) 16

   (B) 25

   (C) 51

   (D) 100

Answers and Explanations

1. **A.** The radius of the circle is also half the length of the square surrounding the circle. Multiply the radius times two (30), and then square that to get the total area of the square (900). Then figure out the area of the circle $A = \pi r^2 = 3.14(15 \times 15) = 3.14 \times 225 = 706.5$. Finally, subtract the two areas to come up with 193.5.

2. **C.** A really simple way to answer this is to figure out which answer choice has two second terms whose sum or difference equals 12. The only one that does this is answer C.

3. **B.** This is a great problem to plug your answer choices into the variable. However, you have to simplify the equation first using order of operations:

$$(12-3)^2 + (\frac{6}{3}) - (\sqrt{49}) = \frac{380}{x}$$

$$(9)^2 + (2) - (7) = \frac{380}{x}$$

$$81 + 2 - 7 = \frac{380}{x}$$

$$76 = \frac{380}{x}$$

Now that you're dealing with a much less scary problem, substitute the answer choices for x, and you'll find that B is correct.

4. **B.** If you remember in Chapter 6, a prime number is divisible by only 1 and itself, making the correct answer B. 6 is divisible by 1, 2, 3, and 6.

5. **B.** First, figure out the height, which is side a. Use the Pythagorean Theorem to calculate this:

$$a^2 + b^2 = c^2$$

$$a^2 + 12^2 = 20^2$$

$$a^2 + 144 = 400$$

$$a^2 = 400 - 144$$

$$a^2 = \sqrt{256} = 16$$

$$a^2 = 16$$

$$a = 4$$

Since you know your height and base, use these numbers to calculate the area:

$$A = \frac{1}{2}bh$$

$$A = \frac{1}{2} \times 12 \times 4$$

$$A = \frac{1}{2} \times 48$$

$$A = \frac{192}{2} = 24$$

Because the question asks what the area is most nearly, your answer is clearly B.

What we've covered in this chapter is hardly exhaustive of the types of math you'll be tested on the Mathematics Knowledge section of the ASVAB, but it's a good start. As always, practice, practice, practice!

Chapter 8

Sir, General Science, Sir!

In This Chapter

- Why you're tested on this
- Essential life, earth, and physical science review
- Tools to help you answer questions correctly.

Did you know that Thomas Edison invented a helicopter that was powered by gunpowder? However, his experiment went up in flames and took his whole factory with it! Sometimes science experiments have to be repeated many times before the results are clear. Life is a lot like a science experiment; after enough trial and error, we start to learn what works and what doesn't.

In this chapter, we explain why the military looks for an aptitude in science for specific jobs, review the basic science concepts you're most likely to encounter on the ASVAB, and provide you with numerous chances to test your knowledge. We've also designed this chapter to minimize the "trial and error" experience in favor of successful results!

Why Do I Have to Take This?

Many military jobs are more technical and dangerous than those you'd encounter as a civilian. And while you will receive specialty training in your military job after boot camp, each branch wants to make sure you have some measure of ability before training begins.

The Army alone has more than 100 jobs that require a basic awareness of scientific concepts. Many of them you would expect, such as engineering or munitions positions. Others may surprise you. Did you know that a Multimedia Illustrator requires science knowledge? Firefighters, military police officers, Psychological Operations Specialists, and Laundry and Shower Specialists also have to receive certain scores on the General Science (GS) section of the ASVAB. (Yes, the Army actually has a job called Laundry and Shower Specialist!)

The bottom line is that if you have a particular job that you want to qualify for, your best bet is to find out which sections of the ASVAB you have to score well on and then concentrate on making the grade. Our review and practice sections will help get you shipshape in no time.

What to Expect

Practically speaking, *science* is all around us; we use it when we're cooking, when our children get sick and we take their temperature, when we scrutinize dark clouds to see if a storm is approaching, when we lift something heavy, and so forth. Throughout this chapter, you will learn how to apply much of the knowledge you already possess to multiple choice–style questions.

def•i•ni•tion

Science refers to a system of acquiring knowledge using observation and experimentation.

Depending on which version of the ASVAB you take, you'll have either 16 (CAT) or 25 (PAP) questions that cover a range of scientific topics, including life, earth, and physical sciences, with some chemistry and astronomy thrown in for good measure.

No matter which version you take, the General Science section of the ASVAB tests your knowledge of life, physical, and earth sciences. The best way to prepare for this and any of the ASVAB technical subtests is to review the material and complete practice questions. So let's get to it!

Life Science

Life science deals with basic biology, cellular biology, health, and nutrition. We break each of these down for you one by one.

Basic Biology

Biological science addresses the structure, function, growth, origin, evolution, distribution, and classification of all living things. It is typically grouped by the type of species being studied. For example, zoology is the study of animals, botany is the study of plants, and microbiology is the study of microorganisms.

Biological classification (taxonomy) is a method by which scientists classify living things. Familiarity with some general taxonomic structures is a must-know for this section of the test. Most living organisms can be divided into the following classifications (listed largest to smallest): kingdom, phylum, class, order, family, genus, and species.

Dogs, for example, are members of the animal kingdom. Kingdom is the broadest classification, and each category that follows gets a bit more focused. Moving most of the way down the list, dogs are further classified into a genus called Canis. The Canis genus includes dogs, coyotes, and wolves, among others. Finally, domestic dogs are further distinguished from all other animals by being placed in their own category, called species. The domestic dog species is called Familiaris. Only members of the same species meet in the wild and mate to produce fertile offspring.

Historically, the kingdom classification includes five categories: Animalia, Plantae, Fungi, Protista, and Monera. Over the years, however, scientists have made numerous changes to the number and classification of these categories.

Cellular Biology

Everything you study in biology is made up of cells, the basis of all life on Earth. Cellular biology examines cell structure. Cells contain all the genetic material necessary for survival and reproduction. Keep in mind that when we say "reproduction," we're not talking about making babies—we're talking about more cells.

Since there are a lot of different types of cells, each with its own special purpose, it's lucky that the ASVAB wants you to know only a few general things about them. Essentials include these:

- **Nucleus:** Part of a eukaryotic cell (one from a complex organism) that contains all the genetic information in the form of DNA (deoxyribonucleic acid) and various proteins. Think of it as the brain of the cell; it controls everything.

- **Mitosis:** The process of dividing one cell into two cells, each with a complete nuclei. This is the simplest form of cell division and results in two identical cells. All cells except those involved with sexual reproduction use this method.

- **Meiosis:** More complex method of cell reproduction that halves the number of chromosomes per cell. The result is either a gamete (cell used in sexual reproduction) or a spore.

Classified Intel

Your body undergoes mitosis every time you get a cut and new skin grows back. Or when your children pull each others' hair, it grows back because of mitosis.

Health

Most health-related questions on the ASVAB deal with systems within the human body. A few you should know about include these:

- **Circulatory system:** Includes all the organs involved with circulating blood throughout the body. Main components are the heart, blood, and blood vessels. Also includes pulmonary circulation, which carries blood through the lungs to oxygenate it before being pumped by the heart out to the rest of the body.

- **Nervous system:** Carries electrical signals throughout the body. Two main parts are the central (brain and spinal cord) and peripheral (nerves that run throughout the body) nervous systems.

- **Digestive system:** System that breaks down food, turns it into energy, and extracts nutrients. Includes the mouth, throat, esophagus (food tube), stomach, liver, gallbladder, intestines, rectum, and anus. These last three also make up the excretory system, which removes waste products from the body.

Nutrition

You may also see questions about the composition of food, how the body processes different types of nutrients, and the function of vitamins and minerals. Keep in mind that you don't have to know everything about these subjects, although you may know more than you realize.

Some general definitions you should be familiar with include these:

- **Proteins:** Nutrients that contains amino acids necessary for tissue growth and repair. Can be found in meats, dairy products, grains, and vegetables.

- **Carbohydrates:** Nutrient made up of varying combinations of sugars that need to be broken down by the body to provide energy to cells.

- **Fats:** Nutrient made up of different types of fatty acids. Saturated (for example, butter and animal fats), polyunsaturated (for example, cottonseed and sesame oils), and monounsaturated (for example, olive and peanut oils) are most common.

When you answer questions about nutrition and health, think back to the labels on your cereal boxes and your trips to the grocery store to make connections between the questions you're asked and what you know. And if all else fails, remember the tips you learned in Chapter 3 to help you eliminate incorrect answer choices!

Test Tip

If you're not sure what a word means, see if smaller words within can give you a clue to its meaning.

Earth Science

Earth science is the study of planet Earth. The ASVAB usually concentrates its questions on astronomy, geology, and meteorology.

Astronomy

Astronomy is the science of celestial bodies and their interactions in space. Examples of this include the structure of the solar system, planets, comets, asteroids, and meteors. Astronomers also examine Earth's shape and structure, how Earth functions within the solar system, concepts of time measurement, composition and features of the moon, and so on.

Basic concepts of astronomy include these:

- **Eclipse:** Comes in two types. With a solar eclipse, the moon comes between Earth and the sun, temporarily casting Earth in shadow. With a lunar eclipse, the moon passes behind Earth, which blocks sunlight from the moon and casts it in shadow.

- **Planets:** Nine planets are in our solar system, which is located in the Milky Way galaxy. Know the order: Mercury, Venus, Earth, Mars, Jupiter, Saturn, Uranus, Neptune, and Pluto. An easy way to remember the planets in order is to use the following mnemonic: "My Very Educated Mother Just Served Us Nine Pizzas."

- **Moons:** Orbit planets, whereas planets orbit the sun. Moons and planets have a gravitational effect on each other. With Earth, the moon's gravity creates ocean tides.

Geology

This branch literally deals with structures of Earth. Most people think simply of rocks when they hear the word *geology*, and to a certain extent, they're right. But really, geology encompasses any liquid or solid form of matter that makes up the planet. You should be familiar with the following:

- **Earth's structure:** Earth is made up of three main layers. These are the crust (what we live on), the mantle (sometimes divided into upper and lower), and the core (has a liquid outer and a solid inner sections).

- **Magma:** This is molten rock when it flows under Earth's surface. Once it reaches topside, it's called lava.

- **Rocks:** Three main types found on Earth are igneous (formed from magma), sedimentary (formed by layers of mineral deposits over time), and metamorphic (one that's changed from one form to another). Hardness is measured on the Mohs Scale of Mineral Hardness.

Meteorology

Despite what you may think about the accuracy of your local weatherperson, meteorology is a legitimate division of earth science. It's the study of the atmosphere, including weather patterns, air pressure, clouds, and temperature. Here are some basics to know:

- **Atmosphere:** Collection of layers containing various gases that sustain life on Earth. Gases include ozone, oxygen, nitrogen, carbon dioxide, and argon. Layers (from inner to outer) are troposphere, stratosphere, mesosphere, ionosphere, and exosphere.

- **Barometric pressure:** Weight of the air pushing down on an area of Earth. High or rising pressure indicates good weather. Low or falling pressure indicates rain or a storm.

- **Clouds:** Visible formations of water vapor that has evaporated from Earth and has settled in the atmosphere. Main types are cumulus (puffy, often in groups), cirrus (wispy, made of ice crystals), cumulonimbus (tall, thick, often bringing thunderstorms), and stratus (uniform in color and density, like a blanket is covering the sky).

Physical Science

The third category of science you will see on the ASVAB is physical science. The two major sub-topics of physical science include chemistry and physics.

Chemistry

By nature, chemistry connects to the other natural sciences, such as astronomy, physics, material science, biology, and geology. It deals with the basic particles of the universe.

You probably remember the periodic table of elements from high school or the properties of water solutions with regard to acids, bases, acid–base reactions, and so forth. It's time to brush up on those long-forgotten elements:

- **Atom:** Basic unit of matter that consists of a nucleus of positively charged protons and uncharged neutrons and a shell of negatively charged electrons.

- **Periodic table:** Structured listing of one-atom chemical elements found in nature. Each is assigned an atomic number that reflects the number of protons in the nucleus. Ninety-two out of 117 elements are metals. There are only 12 nonmetals and 5 metalloids.

Physics

Physics is a set of laws by which other natural sciences abide. Perhaps you recall the phrase, "For every action, there is an equal and opposite reaction." This is one of the famous Sir Isaac Newton's laws. He had three very well-known theories, known as Newton's laws. The ASVAB tests your knowledge of these laws, as well as the concepts behind gravity, weight and mass, energy and heat, conduction, electricity, magnetism, properties of light, and more. Get comfy with the following (we discuss Newton's laws in more detail in Chapter 11):

- **Law of inertia:** Newton's first law states that objects at rest or in motion will remain that way until an unbalanced force acts upon them to change that state. According to this law, a pinwheel will never move until an outside force, such as a breeze, comes in contact with it.

- **Law of motion:** Newton's second law states that the amount of force used to propel an object is proportional to its rate of acceleration (rate that an object's speed increases).

- **Law of reciprocal action:** As we mentioned earlier, Newton's third law states that for every action there is an equal and opposite reaction. Since the term "give-and-take" is synonymous with "reciprical," you should be able to remember this law with ease!

- **Matter:** This is anything that has physical substance or properties, as well as mass.

- **Gravity:** Newton theorized that what goes up must come down. With this, he effectively verbalized gravity, which is the force that pulls all matter toward the center of Earth.

- **Magnetism:** This refers to natural forces that have either attractive or repellent effects on matter. Though we think of metals when we think of magnetism, all matter on Earth is affected in some way by the planet's various magnetic fields.

Practice Questions

Now that you've gotten in some good review, here's your chance to experiment with the next few questions and rate your scientific knowledge.

1. Which of the following falls between order and genus in a biological classification?

   (A) kingdom

   (B) phylum

   (C) family

   (D) species

2. As a free-falling object approaches Earth, its rate of speed

   (A) remains the same.

   (B) slows down.

   (C) accelerates.

   (D) varies.

3. Which one of these is NOT one of the three primary types of rocks found on Earth's surface?

    (A) igneous

    (B) sedimentary

    (C) metamorphic

    (D) basalt

4. What is the hardest substance known?

    (A) topaz

    (B) quartz

    (C) diamonds

    (D) calcite

5. Which body system is in charge of regulating growth, hormones, and metabolism, and helps determine mood?

    (A) musculoskeletal system

    (B) nervous system

    (C) digestive system

    (D) endocrine system

Answers and Explanations

1. **C.** The order of classification is kingdom, phylum, class, order, family, genus, and species.

2. **C.** The longer an object is falling, the more speed it obtains.

3. **D.** Igneous rock is created by magma. Sedimentary rocks are formed over time

by minerals that layer on top of each other. Metamorphic rock is a rock that has transformed from one type to another by heat and pressure. Basalt is a type of igneous rock known as volcanic rock.

4. **C.** On the Mohs Scale of Mineral Hardness, calcite is only a 3. Quartz and topaz are 7 and 8, respectively. Diamonds top the scale, at 10.

5. **D.** Even if you didn't know which system was correct, you could figure out the correct answer. Choice A is wrong because, as the name suggests, the musculoskeletal system consists of bones, muscles, tendons, and ligaments. Choice B is wrong because the nervous system regulates the body's response to internal and external stimuli. Choice C is wrong because the digestive system processes food and turns it into energy.

Before you start to feel overwhelmed by all this information, take a breath and relax. The General Science section has only 16–25 questions. That means each subtopic touches only on basic knowledge, not fine points. Our advice is to take as many practice tests as you can to avoid feeling nervous.

The Electronics Connection

In This Chapter

- Why you're tested on this
- Basic electronics terminology and equations
- Tools to help you answer questions correctly

As the world continues to evolve through the age of information technology, the use of personal electronic devices is also on the rise. When you think about all these miraculous little devices that make our lives *so much* easier (or not), it's hard to believe that they actually employ many fairly basic electronics principles: circuit systems, currents, magnetism, and so on. While the ASVAB will not ask you questions about how to build a DVD player, it will test you on the same basics that drive our growing reliance on electronics.

This chapter gives you a good understanding of the kinds of electronics questions you might find on the ASVAB, reviews the terms and theories often seen on the test, and tells you how best to prepare for this section.

Why Do I Have to Take This?

In the civilian sector, as in the military, electronics is a diverse and growing career field that constantly needs skilled workers, making it an ideal career to begin in the military. In fact, technology and electrical work are as much a part of the modern military as a set of fatigues and a pair of boots.

Classified Intel

Dozens of jobs in the electronics field require knowledge similar to that of an electrician: heating and air-conditioning technicians, refrigeration mechanics and installers, line installers and repairers, electrical and electronics installers and repairers, and elevator installers and repairers.

Of all the technical subtests on the ASVAB, the Electronics Information (EI) section is particularly important to the modern military. Every branch has bragging rights to technological advancements unparalleled by their civilian counterparts.

You could be involved with encoding and decoding messages between ships, or you could be performing maintenance on, and assembling, mines. Yes, mines require maintenance for proper operation, too. If that's a little too much excitement, you might select a job ensuring the accuracy of guided missiles and torpedoes, analyzing electronic intelligence using computer databases, or repairing aviation systems using the latest test equipment and procedures.

The beauty of beginning your electronics career in the military is that you will receive top-notch training in an academic environment, while receiving a comfortable paycheck—right from day one. If you decide to pursue a degree when your service is over, the coursework you completed can transfer into college credits within a network of more than 1,800 colleges nationwide. You'll also receive extensive on-the-job training with communications systems and highly sophisticated, computerized equipment.

In short, scoring well on the electronics section of the ASVAB is your key to an exciting career that's loaded with military excitement and civilian job growth later.

What to Expect

The electronics subtest consists of questions that test your basic knowledge of terminology and equations regarding electricity, wiring, and electrical systems.

The test questions are pretty straightforward, asking you specifics about general and applied concepts. Expect to see questions about circuits, voltage, and grounding. You'll also see questions on amplitude and frequency, sound waves, inductors, and AM radio signals.

Knowing the answers here isn't enough. You have to be quick about it as well. Be prepared to answer 16 questions in eight minutes on the CAT, or 20 questions in nine minutes on the PAP. Our general test tips in Chapter 3 should see you through choosing the best answers for these questions.

Test Tip

Vocab matters, even in the electronics section of the ASVAB. Use the root word and prefix breakdowns from Chapter 4 to try to figure out terms you're not familiar with. Also bone up on the definitions we outline in this chapter.

With the electronics section of the ASVAB, you either know your stuff or you don't. If you're the kind of person who saves the power cord from a broken toaster to use later, or stashes more spare computer parts than a repair shop, a lot of this will be review. If not, this chapter will help you get through the section relatively unscathed.

All About Electricity

When it comes to the language of electronics, the following table defines a few terms you should know before you go any further.

Must-Know Terms

Term	Definition
Electricity	Flow of electrons through a conductor, such as copper or aluminum wire
Conductor	A material through which electricity can pass
Current (I)	Flow of electricity through a conductor
Ampere (A)	Measure of current
Insulator	Something through which electricity can't pass
Voltage	Strength with which current flows through a conductor
Volt (V)	Measure of voltage
Resistance	Hindrance to electric flow
Ohm (Ω)	Measure of resistance
Power (P)	Amount of energy transferred during a specified time
Watt (W)	Measure of electric power

We start our electricity lesson with currents, which is essentially harnessed electricity that flows from one place to another through a conductor. Conductors include almost any metal, such as iron, gold, silver, copper, or mercury. Most household wiring uses copper and is covered with an insulator, such as rubber, to make handling such wires possible.

To understand the concept of "flow," picture two funnels. The first funnel has a very wide spout, therefore allowing a great amount of water to pass through at one time. The second funnel has a very narrow spout, enabling only a sliver of water to pass through. If you placed the two funnels side by side and poured water into them, you would see far more water per second passing through the larger-spouted funnel than the smaller spout.

In the same way, some household appliances, such as hair dryers and microwaves, require more current than other appliances, such as nightlights and alarm clocks. Current is measured in amperes (or amps for short).

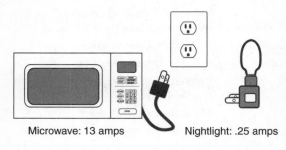

Microwave: 13 amps   Nightlight: .25 amps

When you're looking to find how much electrical force a power source applies, you're looking for the voltage, which is measured in volts. Think of this as the amount of force pushing the current through a conductor. If you pushed the water through the smaller funnel spout discussed earlier instead of just letting it flow naturally, you would increase the speed and force at which it exits the funnel.

The same idea can be applied to currents flowing from a power source, such as the electric company, a gas-powered generator, or a battery. Each produces and sends out a certain amount of voltage, which pushes current along a conductor at a certain rate. Voltage in the United States is fairly standard for most homes. Household fixtures (such as lamps, televisions, or vacuum cleaners) typically run on 120 volts, while some larger appliances, such as ranges or air-conditioners, need 240 volts.

Anything that impedes the flow of a current is called resistance. Most often seen in circuits (discussed later in the chapter), resistance can be just about anything. Resistance is measured in ohms.

Classified Intel

The saying "I could do that with one hand tied behind my back" actually comes from the electronics field. Electricians recommend placing one hand in a back pocket ("tying it behind your back") when working with live wires, so as to stop the flow of electricity in the event of a shock.

Ohm's Law

With a basic understanding of voltage and current, you can understand how all of this is applied. Ohm's law is a good place to start because it defines the proportional relationship among currents, voltage, and resistance within a circuit.

Basically, Ohm's law will get you through a good number of ASVAB questions in this section.

Memorize these simple equations and use them to calculate any of the following.

Related Ohm's Law Equations

Value Sought	Equation	Translation
Ampere (A)	$A = \dfrac{V}{\Omega}$	Amps $= \dfrac{\text{Volts}}{\text{Resistance}}$
Watts (W)	$W = V \times A$	watts = volts × amps
Voltage (V)	$V = A \times \Omega$	volts = amps × ohms
Ohms (Ω)	$\Omega = \dfrac{V}{A}$	Ohms $= \dfrac{\text{Volts}}{\text{Amps}}$

Let's practice a few questions using these equations.

1. You're building a circuit that has a voltage of 120. You add in a resistor of 40 ohms. What is your amperage?

   (A) 3

   (B) 6

   (C) 8

   (D) 10

   Using Ohm's law, you divide your voltage (120) by your resistance (40) and come up with answer A (3).

2. What would your power be if you have 3 amps and 120 volts?

   (A) 40 watts

   (B) 120 watts

   (C) 250 watts

   (D) 360 watts

If you know that your voltage is 120 volts and your current is 3 amps, you would discover that your power usage was 360 watts. (Power = 120 × 3)

Test Tip

Make sure you know the difference between power, amp, current, ohm, volt, watt, and resistance. You'll see these terms in test questions.

Now that you understand the difference between ohms, volts, and watts, you should also know the following related terms:

- **Ohmmeter:** A mechanism used to measure resistance
- **Voltmeter:** A device used to measure the difference in voltage
- **Wattmeter:** A machine used to measure power
- **Ammeter:** A device used to measure current

The Great Circuit Route

With the basics down, let's up the ante and talk about how electric current moves. Not all currents flow the same way. Alternating current (AC) and direct current (DC) describe the two types of currents that flow from sources of power.

AC flows in both directions, reversing itself multiple times per second. It is commonly used by the power company for industrial and domestic customers alike. DC currents travel in only one direction: from power source to destination. Batteries are a common example of DC currents.

When a current flows through a system of conductors, you have a circuit. It's a good idea to acquaint yourself with the following terms before getting into the specifics.

Must-Know Terms

Term	Definition
Circuit	A system of connected conductors that direct the path of electricity
Load	Part of a circuit that converts one type of energy to another (for example, electric to kinetic energy)
Resistor	An electrical device that resists the flow of current; it can also change the amount of current or voltage that's traveling through

Your basic circuit starts with a power source that generates a negative electric current, which then flows through a conductor until it meets a positive charge that closes the circuit. Along the way, it can meet resistors (which raise or lower the voltage or amps of the current), loads (which convert the electric energy into another form—basically, what you're powering), or other components that can change the path of the energy.

Heads-Up

When you see movement from positive to negative on a circuit diagram, you're seeing the flow of current. Electrons, which carry electric energy, move from negative to positive in a circuit. In other words, current and electrons actually flow in opposite directions.

Circuits are generally expressed in diagrams, such as the one here:

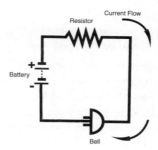

Circuit diagrams are written in symbols. Common examples that are often seen on the ASVAB include these:

Of the circuit symbols in the previous figure, you should familiarize yourself with one symbol in particular: the diode. This circuit component is sort of like an arrow sign indicating a one-way street. Traffic responds to the sign by flowing in only one direction on a one-way street, which helps limit excess movement of cars, trucks, and other vehicles.

Likewise, a diode allows electrical current to flow in one direction, but blocks it from traveling in the opposite direction. Most diodes are made of silicon and have a variety of functions. For one thing, they can be used as light sensors and emitters called light emitting diodes (LEDs).

Classified Intel

LED lights are commonly used in the lettering on restaurants and storefronts. They are also found in the numbers on clocks and the illumination of traffic lights.

Diodes can also convert AC currents to DC currents in a process known as *rectification*. The alternator in your car (which uses the energy produced from your engine to charge your battery) is a good example of a diode that converts AC to DC.

Frequency and Other Essentials

In addition to the basic concepts regarding power and electricity, the ASVAB will ask questions pertaining to frequency, waves, and principles thereof.

Frequency can be applied to both electricity and waves. It's simply a measurement of how many times something is done within a certain amount of time and is expressed in Hertz (Hz). In a circuit, it shows how many times the current completes the one full "lap" per second. With waves, it's how many times it crests in a portion of the wave per second.

To understand frequency better, imagine the Army's physical fitness test. During the first event, each soldier must complete as many push-ups as possible in 2 minutes. Let's say that Private Snuffy completes 60 push-ups in 2 minutes. His frequency would be 0.5 Hz in the given period of time because he completes 1 push-up every 2 seconds.

When you picture any kind of wave, envision a never-ending letter S rotated 90°. Waves are measured in wavelengths, which measure the distance from one peak or crest of a wave to the next corresponding peak or crest.

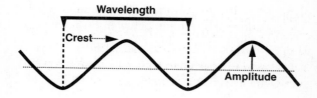

The main calculations you should know for the ASVAB are frequency, amplitude, and wave speed:

- **Frequency:** Measure the full shape of the *S*. By traveling from the beginning to the end of the *S* shape, you have calculated one oscillation, or one Hz of frequency. Counting the number of crests in a specified portion of a wave is an easy way to find the frequency. If you don't have a wave to look at, divide the number of times the event occurs by the amount of time given. Your frequency is then $1/T$, where T is the amount of time that elapsed during the oscillation.

- **Amplitude:** This measures the height of the wave. It's calculated by slicing a line down the middle of the *S*. You then measure from the midline to the top of a crest to determine amplitude.

- **Wave speed:** When you need to calculate how fast a wave is traveling, simply multiply the wavelength measure by the frequency.

Practice Questions

Let's get to the good stuff: the test questions. Using the equations and terminology you just reviewed, select the best answer choice for each question.

1. Most household appliances run on how many volts?

    (A) 120

    (B) 105

    (C) 280

    (D) 400

2. Amps are used to measure

   (A) voltage.

   (B) resistance.

   (C) current.

   (D) circuits.

3. Which of the following is not a good way to describe a diode?

   (A) an arrow for a one-way street

   (B) a telephone that can make outgoing calls and receive incoming calls

   (C) a valve that allows water to flow in one direction

   (D) a turnstile at a railroad station that allows you to enter but not exit through it

4. A wattmeter is a device used for measuring

   (A) power

   (B) amps

   (C) voltage

   (D) induction

5. A sound vibrates 120 times per minute. What is the frequency per second?

   (A) 120 Hz

   (B) 120 ohms

   (C) 2 Hz

   (D) 2 ohms

Answers and Explanations

1. **A.** Some major appliances, such as a range or an air-conditioner, run on 240 volts, but most American appliances run on 120.

2. **C.** Current is measured in amperes, or amps. Voltage is measured in volts; resistance is measured in ohms. Circuits are the loops on which electricity travels from the power source, through the wires, to the fixtures or devices, and back again.

3. **B.** Diodes cause electric current to travel in one direction only, as in the illustrations of choices A, C, and D.

4. **A.** Ammeters measure current, or amps. Voltmeters measure the difference in voltage.

5. **C.** Frequency is measured in Hertz, not ohms. If a minute is 60 seconds long and you want to find out how many frequencies the sound makes per second, you divide the total number of frequencies (120) by the total number of seconds (60). The answer, then, is 2 Hz.

Overall, with the electronics section of the ASVAB, it's ideal to spend a few weeks going over the basic principles that are often seen on the test and completing as many practice questions as possible. Also remember to eliminate any answer choices that you know are wrong before making your final selection—and always check your math!

Chapter 10

Auto/Shop Class

In This Chapter

- Why you're tested on this
- Basic auto systems and how they work
- Review of basic tools
- Practice questions, answers, and explanations

"A slipping gear could let your M203 grenade launcher fire when you least expect it. That would make you quite unpopular in what's left of your unit." —*PS Magazine*

Although this excerpt from the Army's monthly maintenance magazine is phrased humorously, the subject itself is quite serious. It's a good reminder that the same skills used by civilians can also be implemented by service members in far different ways, and with far different consequences.

This chapter introduces you to some of the various automotive- and maintenance-related topics that are often seen in the Automotive and Shop Information (AS) section of the ASVAB.

Why Do I Have to Take This?

A variety of careers in all five branches of service offer automotive and shop jobs. Furthermore, this kind of military work often translates nicely into a civilian job later. For example, a Motor Transporter in the Marine Corps may perform mechanical maintenance and body repair to motor vehicles and amphibious trucks alike. When their time in the service is up, they could then pursue work as an auto or body mechanic, a builder of custom vehicles, or even an auto shop teacher.

Although a Motor Transporter would be trained to perform mechanical work after entering the service, someone looking to land this particular job would have to show a certain aptitude for it prior to enlistment. That's what this section of the ASVAB assesses.

What to Expect

As with most of the technical sections of the ASVAB, the AS subtest features "you know it or you don't" types of questions. This section (like all the sections of the ASVAB) is also different depending on which version of the test you take. With the PAP, you have to answer 25 auto and shop questions in 11 minutes. However, on the CAT, the test is divided into separate sections. The Automotive Information section is 11 questions in 7 minutes, and the Shop Information section is 11 questions in 6 minutes. Your score report will list the total score of both under the AS category.

Our goal in this chapter is to expand on the practical knowledge you already have so that you can effectively apply it to multiple-choice questions. Let's begin by examining some of your car's major operating systems and the general maintenance that corresponds to a few major ones.

Automotive Review

We love our cars. They're one of the most convenient inventions of the last 150 years. Most of us know something about how our cars work:

- The brakes make the car slow or stop.
- The battery supplies power for certain functions, like starting the car, using the radio, and unlocking the doors.
- The exhaust system takes excess gases from the engine and releases them into the air.
- The suspension system deals with the movement of the wheels and how the car reacts to terrain.
- The engine runs on gasoline and needs oil to keep all its moving parts working properly.
- The electrical system makes the lights and power systems work.
- You need coolant to keep the engine temperature at a certain level.

All of this is great stuff to know walking into the ASVAB. Much of this will help you reason out answers to questions you may not know the exact answer for, through a little process of elimination. Now let's look at a few key systems in a little more depth.

The Brake System

When you are speeding down the highway, your vehicle's ability to stop when you need it to is crucial. Knowing how this actually works is also good when you take the ASVAB.

Generally, modern cars are designed with front- and rear-wheel disc brakes. Some vehicles still have drum brakes on the rear wheels, though. It's important to know how both work:

- **Disc brakes:** These consist of brake pads, rotors, and calipers. Brake pads aren't the cushy type of pads that may come to mind when hearing the word. They're metallic blocks that apply friction to both sides of the disc brake. Newer-style pads can also be made from ceramics and other materials.

Disc Brake

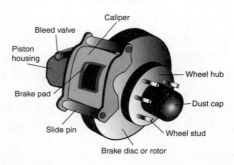

Rotors are made of machined steel and are mounted to the hub. The hub allows the car to turn and the wheels to spin.

Calipers house the brake pads and are mounted so that they straddle the rotor. The caliper contains at least one piston. When you press the brake pedal, hydraulic pressure (fluid power) is exerted on the piston, which then forces the pad against the rotor. Friction between the pads and the rotors (which are sometimes referred to as discs) causes the car to slow down.

- **Drum brakes:** As we discussed earlier, many vehicles still have drum brakes. These function similarly to disc brakes, even though they are made of different parts: a backing plate, brake shoes, a brake drum, and a wheel cylinder.

The backing plate (or mounting plate) is where each of the drum elements is attached. Brake shoes can be functionally compared to the brake pads from the disc system. The main difference is that whereas the brake pads are flat, the shoes are curved and push out instead of in.

The brake drum is a hollow metal cylinder that is attached to the wheel. It fits snugly around the brake shoes so that when the shoes press against it, this causes the friction that slows the vehicle.

The wheel cylinder is located at the top of the backing plate. It houses two pistons, one on either side. When you step on the brake, hydraulic fluid forces each piston out of the cylinder. The pistons are slotted at the end so that the shoe fits into their groove. When you take your foot off the brake, they are then retracted by a set of springs into the cylinder so that they're ready to perform the whole process all over again.

Like disc brakes, drum brakes have a small metal clip to alert the driver that the shoes are getting worn and should be replaced.

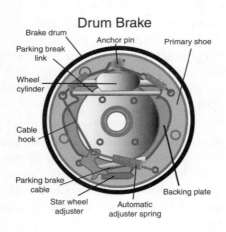

Drum Brake

The Cooling System

The cooling system is aptly named because its primary function is to keep the engine cool. Most modern cooling systems use fluids that circulate throughout the engine to keep the temperature down. This system has several key components that allow it do its job, including a water pump, a thermostat, and a radiator.

The water pump simply provides the pressure needed to circulate coolant through the cavities of the engine. Much like your home has a thermostat to control the air temperature, a vehicle has a thermostat to help control the temperature of the engine. It does this by opening and closing a valve to allow and stop the flow of coolant to the engine.

Occasionally, the thermostat malfunctions, which can have a variety of consequences depending on the nature of the problem. If the thermostat gets stuck in the open position, for example, the engine won't heat up to the proper temperature. Conversely, if the thermostat gets stuck in the closed position, the engine will overheat. If either situation goes undetected, the engine can be damaged.

The radiator reduces the temperature of the coolant after it exits the engine and is probably the most well-known element of the cooling system. It consists of a parallel network of small tubes through which the hot fluid flows. This fluid faces a fan system that forces cool air through the radiator, thereby helping to cool the fluid.

In short, the cooling system functions basically as follows: the water pump pushes cool fluid through the engine; the engine causes the cool fluid to become hot; and the now hot fluid exits the engine and flows into the radiator, cools off, and cycles back around to the water pump.

Cooling System

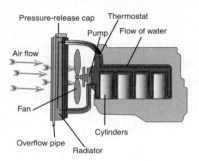

The Ignition and Starting Systems

The ignition and starting systems work together to start your car. The specific elements that comprise these systems have changed significantly over the years with the advent of computer technology. Because some of the ASVAB questions still ask about distributors and other precursors to computerized ignition systems, we'll discuss those as well.

Like the cooling system, the ignition system is a subclassification of the engine system. This is what actually allows your car to start and run, thereby permitting the engine to do its job.

Ever notice how all your dashboard lights (and the radio and AC, when left on) all come to life the second you turn the key, even before you crank the engine? This happens because everything in your car that uses electricity to run is connected to the ignition switch, which acts as an intermediary between the battery and the rest of the car's electrical components.

The battery is your car's initial source of energy. Power from the battery travels to the ignition switch and is held back until you activate the ignition with your key. Then the power flows through the ignition switch to the lights, the ignition coil, the solenoid, and any electrical accessories (like your radio).

Heads-Up

The alternator uses the energy generated by the running of your engine to recharge the battery. When it stops working properly, the battery doesn't get charged, your car won't start, and you can wind up with some hefty towing and mechanic fees!

Starting old and new cars alike involves the following steps:

1. Turning the key to the first position activates the ignition.

2. Power transfers from the battery through the ignition switch to the ignition coil, which sends power to the distributor (if present) and spark plugs.

3. When you turn the key to the next position, you engage the solenoid, a relay that powers the starter motor and turns electrical energy into mechanical energy.

4. Once engaged, the starter motor causes the fly wheel on the engine to turn, which also moves the engine's crankshaft.

5. Rods connected to the crankshaft move the pistons inside the engine up and down.

6. The piston movement draws in air and fuel (regulated by the fuel system).

7. The ignition system ignites the air/fuel mixture on the engine's compression stroke (action of the pistons traveling up and down).

Traditionally, the spark plugs received the battery's voltage through an ignition coil that would boost the voltage along the way. This was a key step in the ignition process because the spark plugs needed to receive enough voltage (tens of thousands of volts, that is!) to ignite the air/fuel mixture. The distributor, which had a replaceable cap and rotor, took the current from the ignition coil and sent it to the spark plugs within each cylinder of the engine via a spark plug wire.

Over the years, however, the addition of electronic control modules (ECMs) has helped to improve efficiency. The single ignition coil has also been replaced by a system of coils in newer cars. In fact, the entire ignition system has been converted to an electronic system in many modern cars, thereby eliminating the distributor and ECM altogether.

Shifting Gears: Shop Review

In the case of the ASVAB, the word *shop* refers to carpentry and other basic handyman subjects. So if you've ever done any home-improvement projects, you'll probably recognize some of the terms in the shop category of this section, including countersink, Phillips and flathead screws, and more.

Hand Tools

Sometimes it seems as though everything has to be supersized, supercharged, and superfast these days; this includes everything from fast food to tools. Nevertheless, quite a few manual tools can really get the job done—and have been known to pop up on the ASVAB.

Drills

Although most modern drills have power of some kind, many woodworkers prefer to use the hand drill. A drill is a tool that has a rotating bit used for boring holes in various materials. On a hand drill, a cranking handle turns the main shaft, thereby rotating the bit at the end of the shaft. The toothed bit is held in place by a chuck.

Screwdrivers

These common shop tools come in many different shapes, sizes, and styles. A screwdriver is used to manually twist a screw into a piece of wood, plastic, or metal. Generally, the purpose is to fasten two materials to one another.

The Phillips head screwdriver is a staple in most homes; it has a pointy, tapered end with an *X* shape at the bottom. This type of screwdriver must be used with a Phillips head screw, which also has an *X* shape on top.

A flathead screwdriver has a single, flat end that fits into a slotted screw. On top of a flathead screw is a single groove into which the screwdriver fits.

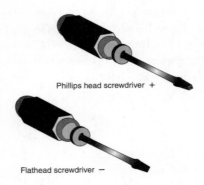

Phillips head screwdriver +

Flathead screwdriver −

Wrenches

These are another common type of hand tool used to hold or twist a nut or bolt. As with screwdrivers, many types of wrenches are available to do different types of jobs.

An adjustable wrench is sometimes called a crescent wrench and is a good example of what your regular, everyday wrench looks like. The width of this wrench can be adjusted to fit the size of the nut you're working with.

A monkey wrench has adjustable jaws with thick teeth that grab onto metal and is used for turning pipes and nuts of varying sizes. It's much bigger than an adjustable wrench.

An Allen wrench is an L-shaped bar with a hexagonal head. It is used to turn Allen screws, which are commonly found in ready-to-finish or -assemble furniture.

A socket wrench (also known as a ratchet) uses separate, removable sockets to tighten different sizes of nuts and bolts. These wrenches are used in automotive repairs, as well as other household projects.

Wrench

Allen wrench

Monkey wrench

Socket wrench

Chisels

Chisels can be used for shaping stone or wood and cutting through some metals. They are thick, flat blades of metal with a handle and a wide sharpened end. The sharp end is placed on the material that is being shaped, while a hammer taps at the end of the handle to push it forward into the wood, stone, or metal. Cold chisels are used on metal. Wood chisels can be used to chip off pieces of wood from a larger piece or smooth out a portion.

Saws

These are thin pieces of metal with jagged edges, used to cut through wood or metal. Different styles have different designs and purposes. For example, a coping saw has a narrow blade with tiny teeth so that it can easily cut into small spaces. A rip saw has a wide blade and large teeth to quickly make large cuts with the grain of the wood.

Power Tools

Let's be honest. Would you rather use a lot of time and muscle to operate a manual screwdriver when you could let the tool do all the work in half the time? Many power tools have really simplified the lives of carpenters, handymen, and the average Joe (or Jane) alike. Important ones to know include drills, saws, routers, and lathes.

Drills

Power drills are handy inventions for cutting holes, just like the hand drill noted earlier. It uses removable bits in a variety of widths depending on the size needed for the hole. In terms of shop usage, drills are used in woodworking, metalworking, construction, and other basic projects. Main types to know include:

- **Pistol grip:** Probably the most common, the pistol grip can be found in both the corded and cordless varieties. It's typically used for standard projects, such as drilling holes in drywall to hang pictures, drilling through wood, and so on.

- **Hammer drill:** This drill uses an action similar to its namesake and is used most frequently in drilling masonry. A jackhammer is an example of a hammer drill.

- **Drill press:** This is a fixed tool that is typically either mounted to a workbench or bolted to the floor. Its main advantages are that it takes even less human effort to operate, and the project can be more securely held in place during the drilling process.

Drill bits are pieces of metal that enable the drill to bore into whatever surface you're using it on. They also vary as much as drills do. Some popular types include

- **Countersink:** This is used to create a hole in which the top part of the hole is enlarged. The purpose is to allow the head of a screw or bolt to lie flush with (or slightly below) the surface of the wood or metal.

- **Twist bit:** This is the most common drill bit and is used to drill through wood, plastic, and metal.

- **Spade bit:** This looks like its name and is used for rough boring through wood.

Power Saws

Many different kinds of power saws exist today, depending on the type of cut needed:

- **Miter saw:** Also called a chop or drop saw, this saw has a circular blade and makes straight cuts on an angle. This is used in making a picture frame, for example. With a compound miter saw, you can change the angle of the blade to cut a beveled edge.
- **Circular saw:** This is one of the most common saws in use today and is used to make straight, continuous cuts. Depending on the blade it's equipped with, it can cut wood, steel, masonry, or ceramic tile.
- **Jigsaw:** When you need to make cuts that are not just straight lines, the jigsaw is what you need. It has a narrow blade that moves vertically in a reciprocating motion and can make intricate cuts and curves.

Practice Questions

Take a moment to test your understanding of auto systems and shop information with the following questions.

1. Which of the following parts is NOT found in disc brakes?

   (A) pads

   (B) rotors

   (C) shoes

   (D) calipers

2. A solenoid belongs to which automotive system?

   (A) brakes

   (B) starting

   (C) exhaust

   (D) coolant

3. When fluid flows through the radiator, it

   (A) heats up.

   (B) cools down.

   (C) stays the same temperature.

   (D) depends on the situation.

4. The best saw to use when making angled, beveled cuts is the

   (A) jigsaw.

   (B) circular saw.

   (C) router.

   (D) compound miter saw.

5. Which type of wrench has a hexagonal-shaped head?

   (A) Phillips head

   (B) monkey wrench

   (C) Allen wrench

   (D) flathead

Answers and Explanations

1. **C.** Shoes are found in drum brakes, not disc brakes.

2. **B.** The solenoid is part of the starter itself and is also known as a relay.

3. **B.** The fan system forces cool air through the radiator, thereby cooling fluid that just came from the hot engine.

4. **D.** A jigsaw makes intricate, curvy cuts; a circular saw makes straight, continuous cuts; and a router is not a saw.

5. **C.** Choices A and D are wrong because they are screwdrivers, not wrenches. A monkey wrench is an adjustable wrench, so choice B is also incorrect.

As you can tell, there's a lot more we could talk about in this section. Check out the resources in the Appendix for a more thorough review.

Get Mechanically Inclined

In This Chapter

- Why you're tested on this
- Basic mechanical terminology and equations
- Tools to help you answer questions correctly

Doing well on the Mechanical Comprehension (MC) subtest can help turn dreams into reality for individuals pursuing careers as skilled technicians. For others, it can open a whole new world of career possibilities. Either way, studying up on this section is a good idea.

This chapter gives you a quick review of concepts often seen in this section of the ASVAB, must-know terms that will help you understand the questions you might see, and some practice questions to get your brain back into the pendulum swing of things.

Why Do I Have to Take This?

Depending on the needs of the military and ASVAB scores, a person straight out of high school could join the military to become an air traffic controller. Following basic training, the service member would complete an FAA-approved ATC course on a military installation. Upon graduation, he or she would become a certified air traffic controller employable by any airport in the country.

Classified Intel

On average, civilian air traffic controllers make more than $117,000 per year. After four years of military service and with no prior education, this isn't a bad starting salary as a civilian!

However, many of the technical and aviation-related jobs in the military require a basic understanding of mechanical principles. This means knowing how to calculate acceleration rates, natural laws governing motion, and other such things.

Mechanical Basics

Like service members, mechanical science has a language all its own. Some of these terms are quite simple, and even someone with no mechanical background would be able to identify them: motion, speed, acceleration, force, energy, work, and so on. Familiarize yourself with the following terms:

Must-Know Terms

Term	Definition
Mass	The amount of matter an object has. Can be measured in kilograms
Matter	Anything that occupies space and has mass
Motion	Any object that changes distance over a period of time
Speed	How fast an object is moving
Velocity	Speed, plus the direction of motion
Acceleration	The rate of change in velocity
Work	Transferring energy through force over a distance
Force	Something that changes an object at rest into an object in motion
Energy	The amount of work a force can produce
Potential energy	Stored energy; an object with the potential to do work
Kinetic energy	Energy of motion

Motion

Motion is simply movement of any kind; it could be something as large as an aircraft carrier slicing through choppy waters or as small as a vibration generated by a bee's wings. To understand motion, you need to gain some knowledge of the law—Newton's law, that is! In Chapter 8, we touched on Sir Isaac Newton and his three essential mechanical laws of motion, which we now explain in more depth.

Newton's First Law

Newton's law of inertia states that objects tend to resist changes in motion. An object in motion tends to stay in motion, and an object at rest tends to stay at rest, unless a force is exerted upon it. This means that nothing that has mass will move without some force making it move. The more mass an object has, the greater the force needed to make it move. Once something has been put in motion, only another force can make it change course (increase speed, change direction, and so on).

It's important to understand the difference between mass and weight. Weight, although similar to mass, measures the amount of gravitational force exerted on an object. If that force is altered—say, by going to the moon—weight changes. The mass of an object, however, is the same anywhere—on Earth, on the moon, and so on—regardless of gravitational pull.

To figure out the mass of an object, you multiply its volume (v) by its density (d): $M = dv$. To calculate weight, you multiply the mass (m) of the object by the gravitational acceleration (force)(g) exerted on the object: $W = mg$.

In the United States, weight is usually expressed in pounds. The metric system expresses weight in Newtons. Most people from other areas of the world measure an object's mass, not its weight. That's why you hear the term *kilograms* more often than *Newtons*.

Newton's Second Law

Newton's law of motion states that the acceleration of an object is directly proportional to the net force acting on the object; in addition, an object accelerates in the direction of the net force acting on it.

So basically, this law talks about the effect a force has on how fast an object moves. To calculate force, you multiply the mass (*m*) of the object by its acceleration (*a*): $F = ma$.

Test Tip

If you have two values for any of the three letters of an equation (as in the previous example), you can solve for the missing value.

Let's use a weight-lifting example to illustrate Newton's second law. Let's say you do a set of bicep curls using a 15-pound single-handed dumbbell, switching from one hand to the other. On the next set, you use the curl bar with both hands, but you still lift 15 pounds total. By using twice as much force (two arms instead of one), you produced twice as much acceleration.

Most likely, though, you would have increased the weight on the curl bar so that you would still get a good workout. Therefore, if you increased the weight on the two-handed curl bar to 30 pounds, you would have had the same acceleration as the single-handed 15-pound dumbbell.

Twice the acceleration on twice the mass gives you the same amount of acceleration. When there is no acceleration, an object is said to be in mechanical equilibrium.

Newton's Third Law

Newton's law of reciprocal action is pretty straight-forward. This is the famous "For every action, there is an equal and opposite reaction" concept that just about everyone learns as a kid.

When you do jumping jacks (also known as "the side straddle hop" in the Army), your feet push against the ground and the ground pushes against you—which you can't even feel. The forces occur simultaneously. However, when you practice water survival training with all your gear on, you push against the force of the water and it pushes against you—which you definitely feel!

Speed

Now that we've talked about motion, let's look at some of the tools used to measure motion. We start with speed, the rate at which an object moves.

If you want to measure the speed of Drill Sergeant Joe's car, and you know that the car has traveled 30 miles in 60 minutes, you can easily determine that the car's speed is $\frac{1}{2}$ mile per minute. Without even realizing it, you just calculated an equation that you can use to measure any speed:

$$\text{Speed} = \frac{\text{Distance}}{\text{Time}}$$

Velocity

Velocity is a measure of both the speed and direction an object moves. If Drill Sergeant Joe has to travel due west from the firing range to the barracks, and he maintains a constant speed of 30 miles per hour, we call that constant velocity because both the speed and the direction of the car are unchanging. But if he gets lost and starts driving in circles, the velocity is no longer constant because the direction is continuously changing.

Acceleration

Speaking of change, what happens when an object speeds up (increases velocity)? In general, this change is known as acceleration (a) and is calculated by subtracting the initial rate of velocity (vi) from the final rate of velocity (vf), and dividing that value by the length of time (t) in which the change occurs: $A = \dfrac{vf - vi}{t}$. The answer is represented in squared units of the measure of velocity, such as miles per second.

Imagine how it feels when an airplane prepares for takeoff. Usually, the pilot positions the plane at the beginning of the runway, pauses for a few seconds, and then hits the gas (so to speak). Your body presses into the seat as the plane accelerates rapidly down the runway. If the plane goes from 0 miles per hour to 30 miles per hour in 2 seconds, you would say that the plane is accelerating 15 miles per second squared ($15\dfrac{mi}{s^2}$).

Likewise, when the plane comes in for a landing and hits the brakes, this is negative acceleration. The same principles apply: if the pilot slows the plane from 200 miles per hour to 10 miles per hour over the course of 5 seconds, after you got over your wicked case of whiplash, you could determine that his negative acceleration was $38\frac{mi}{s^2}$. Change in velocity was 190 miles per hour, divided by a time interval of 5 seconds.

Gravitational Acceleration

When we talked about weight earlier, we introduced you to gravitational acceleration (g). This is a measure of the force gravity has on an object. On Earth, gravitational acceleration is equal to $9.8\frac{m}{s^2}$ or $32.2\frac{ft}{s^2}$.

When an object is allowed to fall with only the force of gravity acting on it (we call this freefalling), the ratio of weight to mass is constant. This means that if a car and a paper clip were dropped without air friction, both would hit the ground at the same time because the ratio of weight to mass is the same for both heavy and light objects.

So apply this knowledge to the following question: will a car and a paper clip fall at the same speed when dropped from a tall building?

The answer is, not quite. Though the car may have more than 500 times the mass of a paper clip, it also has 500 times the force against it, which would theoretically cause them to fall at the same speed.

However, air friction and wind resistance can make for some deviation from this rule. While it is often safe to ignore air friction, it can make a difference, as any paratrooper will tell you.

Work and Energy

Work and energy are intimately connected. Energy is the amount of work a force can produce. Energy has eight main forms, any of which can be converted into another: kinetic, potential, gravitational, electromagnetic, thermal, sound, elastic, and light.

Work is the amount of energy that is transferred through force over distance. When you carry groceries from the store to your car, you are performing work. If you carry two bags, you are doing twice as much work as you would if you had one bag. (It takes twice as much force to carry two bags versus one.)

To figure out total work performed by this action, you multiply the amount of force exerted by the distance traveled: $W = fd$. Check out the following example:

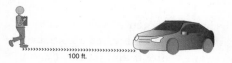

100 ft.

Work = 661 N × 100 ft. = 66,100 joules

200 ft.

Work = 661 N × 200 ft. = 132,200 joules

Carrying one bag 200 feet is twice as much work as carrying one bag 100 feet because you are performing twice as much work if you double the distance that you have to travel. In the previous example, the man's weight and that of the groceries he carries is converted into Newtons (multiply weight in kilograms by gravitational force) as a measure of force. The distance of the car from the store affects the amount of work he has to do travel from store to car.

Test Tip

Work, potential energy, and kinetic energy are all measured in joules.

Now let's take a look at two types of energy often seen on the ASVAB: potential and kinetic.

Potential Energy

Potential energy is related to work because it is assumed that certain objects at rest are capable of doing work (the object has stored energy).

The spring inside the Army's M60 semiautomatic machine gun exemplifies potential energy. The spring is part of the bolt assembly and a key element in the weapon's ability to fire repeatedly. When it's tightly coiled, the spring is at rest and stores elastic energy, which is a type of potential energy. When it's released, the spring discharges energy, thus assisting in the process of automatically firing multiple rounds per second.

To figure out the potential energy of an object, multiply its mass (m) by the gravitational force exerted on it (g) and the distance in meters it is away from the center of the planet (h): $Ep = mgh$.

Kinetic Energy

Kinetic energy, on the other hand, describes the energy inherent to a moving object. A riding lawn mower, when running, possesses kinetic energy. To calculate kinetic energy (in joules), you multiply the object's mass (in kilograms) by its velocity, and then multiply that value by $\frac{1}{2}$:

$$KE = \frac{1}{2}mv^2$$

Using the riding lawn mower example, suppose you work for a landscaping company, and you have a John Deere that weighs 500 kilograms (kg). You are asked to mow a grassy field, which you can do at a rate of 5 kilometers per hour (kph). The competitor has a mower with the same mass, but it can get the job done at 10 kph. Using the previous formula, the competition's mower actually has four times as much kinetic energy as yours does!

The kinetic energy produced by your lawn mower is 6,250 joules ($\frac{1}{2} \times 500 \times 5^2 = \frac{1}{2} \times 500 \times 25 = \frac{1}{2} \times 12500 = \frac{1}{2} \times \frac{12500}{2} = 6250$), while the kinetic energy produced by your competitor's mower is

$$25{,}000 \text{ joules } (\frac{1}{2} \times 500 \times 10^2 = \frac{1}{2} \times 500 \times 100 =$$

$$= \frac{1}{2} \times \frac{50000}{2} = 25000).$$

Gear Ratios

Gear ratios are essential for anyone looking to work with machines to learn and understand. Gears are small wheels with teeth that interlock and turn either other gears or mechanical components. A driving gear is one that is motorized by some force. When its teeth interlock with another gear, the motion from the driving gear turns the second gear in the opposite direction.

Gear Ratios

You can determine the ratio of these two gears by counting their teeth. (See Chapter 6 for more information about ratios.) In the previous figure, the gear on the left has 21 teeth, while the gear on the right has 16 teeth. This makes the gear ratio 21:16.

Why do we need to know this? The gear ratio directly influences the rate at which the two gears turn. Using the previous example, knowing that the gear ratio is 21:16, we know that if the first gear turns once, the second will turn $1\frac{5}{16}$ times.

Pulleys

Pulleys are simple machines that make heavy work a lot easier. A pulley is made up of a grooved wheel attached to an axle that allows the wheel to turn. If you run a rope through the groove and attach the rope to an object, lifting that object becomes easier because you're adding leverage to the force you put into pulling the object. This is called mechanical advantage. Three main types of pulleys include these:

- **Fixed:** The axle is connected to a stationary object.

- **Movable:** The axle here is not attached to anything except the pulley wheel.

- **Compound:** This type of pulley blends several fixed and/or movable pulleys to maximize mechanical advantage. A block and tackle is a common type of compound pulley.

To calculate the mechanical advantage of a pulley, simply count the number of rope sections used in the machine. The compound pulley would be a better choice for lifting heavier objects.

Practice Questions

Now that you know a little bit about the mechanical world, it's time to test your knowledge.

1. A roller coaster flies down the first hill at 50 kilometers per hour. As it starts the assent of the next hill, it decelerates to 15 kilometers per hour within 5 seconds. What is the rate of deceleration?

    (A) $5\dfrac{\text{km}}{\text{s}^2}$

    (B) 5 joules

    (C) $7\dfrac{\text{km}}{\text{s}^2}$

    (D) 7 joules

2. Which two terms are used to measure weight?

    (A) Newtons and kilograms

    (B) Newtons and pounds

    (C) pounds and kilograms

    (D) kilometers and grams

3. If you have to move a package vertically 100 meters using a force of 20 Newtons, how much work will you do?

    (A) 2,000 joules

    (B) 5 joules

    (C) 120 joules

    (D) 200 joules

4. What is the kinetic energy of a car that weighs 800 kilograms and travels at 10 kilometers per hour?

   (A) 8,000 joules

   (B) 40,000 joules

   (C) 80 joules

   (D) 4,000 joules

5. When a magician yanks a tablecloth off a table that is completely set with fine china, none of the china breaks. This is an example of what?

   (A) motion

   (B) equilibrium

   (C) friction

   (D) inertia

Answers and Explanations

1. **C.** The rate of negative acceleration is 35 (50 − 15), which is divided by 5 (seconds it took to slow) equals 7. The deceleration in this case is $\frac{km}{s^2}$. Joules measure work, potential energy, kinetic energy, and heat.

2. **B.** Kilograms are used to measure mass; kilometers and grams are metric measurements for distance and volume, respectively.

3. **A.** Work is measured in joules, and the formula for work is $W = f \times d$, or force times distance. If we plug the numbers from the

question into the formula, we get $20 \times 100 =$ 2,000 joules. The word *vertical* had no bearing on the equation.

4. **B.** The formula for kinetic energy is
   $KE = \frac{1}{2}mv^2$. Therefore, $\frac{1}{2} \times 800 \times 10^2 =$
   $\times 800 \times 100 = \frac{1}{2} \times 80000 = \frac{80000}{2} = 40000$
   or 40,000 joules.

5. **D.** Inertia is the resistance an object has to changing its state of motion. According to Newton's law of inertia, the sudden movement of the tablecloth did not affect the china because it did not exhibit enough force on the china to overcome its natural resistance to change.

You should be able to work through a variety of questions using the information in this chapter, including those with terms or equations that you don't feel completely comfortable with.

Chapter 12

Assembling Objects

In This Chapter

- Why you're tested on this
- Two types of problems that deal with assembling objects
- Sample illustrations and problems

In ancient times (such as the 1980s), people used paper maps to guide them in their travels. But since the Global Positioning System has become more accessible and affordable, small electronic devices of all sorts have begun to take the place of traditional maps.

The main advantage of this is that you don't have to think or take your eyes off the road to read a map, but the downside is that map-reading skills have become less important. Aside from the fact that you'll need to understand and interpret maps in most branches of the service, map reading helps you expand your intellect.

It's true! That old-fashioned piece of paper that you can never refold properly is a good tool to measure and enhance your visual intelligence, which is exactly what the Assembling Objects (AO) section of the ASVAB is designed to assess. This chapter introduces you to this section of the test, breaks down the types of questions you'll see, and shows you how to approach solving these little puzzles.

Why Do I Have to Take This?

The AO subtest measures your spatial and problem-solving abilities. Spatial intelligence basically refers to a person's ability to think visually or abstractly. It requires analytical skills, creativity, and (typically) good communication skills.

Maybe you're wondering why the military cares if you can think "outside the box," so to speak. Well, the answer is quite simple: this type of skill is directly related to your ability to perform a multitude of tasks, such as estimating distances, repairing machinery, and strategizing war.

Classified Intel

As of the writing of this book, the Navy is the only branch of the military that uses the AO scores for job placement. However, sources from the Official ASVAB Enlistment Testing Program say that this will change in the near future. Also, the other branches of the service may use your AO score to gain additional information about your abilities.

What to Expect

You can expect to see the AO subtest on both the CAT and PAP versions of the ASVAB. The CAT version gives you 16 questions to answer in 16 minutes. The PAP version has 25 questions to answer in 15 minutes—a big difference in the number of questions. This section is not used on the high school version of the ASVAB.

You must solve two types of visual problems in this portion of the test: connectors and puzzles. You'll see one example and then have to choose an answer that either shows how two objects are connected or what puzzle pieces would look like when assembled. We take you through these one-by-one next.

AO Problem Type 1: Connectors

This type of problem involves connecting two objects using a straight line. The shape of the objects varies in each question; they could be geometric in nature, letters of the alphabet, or just a random form. Each shape also has a small letter positioned near one corner or one side of the shape.

Your task is to determine how a straight line would connect the two letters on each shape. To do so, you must be able to visually rotate the shapes and imagine how they would look in a different position.

Your answer choices consist of four different illustrations. You must pick the one that represents the new position the two objects would assume if they were connected by a straight line.

Test Tip

Process of elimination is the best strategy for tackling these questions.

Check out the following illustration of an AO connector-type problem:

In the following diagram, which figure best shows how the objects in the first box would touch if points A and B were connected?

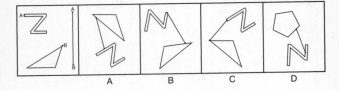

If you selected answer choice C, you made the correct connection. Looking at the original diagram, notice that the small letter *A* is located at the very end of the top shape—the one that looks like the letter Z. Based on this fact, you can rule out choices A and D because the straight-line connector is incorrectly positioned on the Z shape.

Likewise, choice B is incorrect because the small letter *B* is located at one of the triangle's corners instead of on the side, as depicted in answer choice B. That leaves you with choice C.

This type of problem solving may be very unusual for you because it's not something students are commonly tested on in school. The good news is, this is a skill that you can improve with a little practice.

Test Tip

With connector problems, look for an answer that shows each end of the connecting line in the *exact* place shown in the example. If the connection points are shown elsewhere in an answer choice, eliminate it as a possible answer.

Let's look at one more connector problem:

In the following diagram, which figure best shows how the objects in the first box would touch if points A and B were connected?

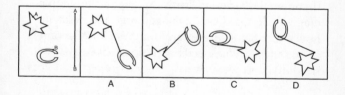

Choice B is the correct answer this time. Again, looking at the positioning of the small letters, you can effectively rule out choices A and D: the small letter *B* is located on the end of the shape that looks like a *C*, not in the middle.

The same is true for C. The line isn't connected at the same part of the star shown in the example, though it's much closer to the correct position than the other choices. This leaves B as the only real choice.

For additional practice, try reading maps and doing some simple sketching. This type of work has proven useful in enhancing a person's visual-spatial skill set.

AO Problem Type II: Puzzles

The second type of question you will encounter on this subtest is the puzzle problem. Essentially, you are given a diagram that looks like pieces of a jigsaw puzzle. Your answer choices show you various versions of those pieces put together to make a whole.

Keep in mind that you're not just trying to make a whole puzzle; you're trying to make a whole puzzle that matches *identically* with the one in the sample diagram. Rotated versions of an object are okay; however, mirror images are not. Why? Reflections of an object are not exact copies, which is what you need in a correct answer.

The following examples show you what we mean about putting the right pieces together:

Which answer choice best shows how the objects in the first box would appear if they were fitted together?

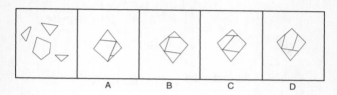

If you selected answer choice B, you completed the puzzle correctly. The pieces in answer A are different sizes than the ones in the example. The pieces in answers C and D are different shapes than those in the example. Again, process of elimination leads you to the correct answer.

Try one more sample puzzle:

Which answer choice best shows how the objects in the first box would appear if they were fitted together?

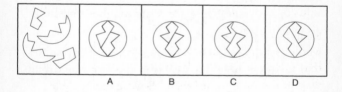

Again, the answer is B. You can eliminate answer C right away because the shapes inside the circle are different from those in the example. The shapes in answer A are not in the same proportion as those in the example. Those in answer D are mirror images of the original shapes, which eliminates them as answer choices.

The best way to get better at this type of question is to practice putting together jigsaw puzzles. Your friends and family may not believe that you're actually studying for a test if they see you leisurely putting together a puzzle, but it works for this type of visual problem!

Heads-Up

Expect the answer choices on this section to show both rotated and mirrored versions of the objects in the example. Whenever you see a mirror image in an answer choice, you know it isn't a correct answer.

Practice Questions

The old adage that practice makes perfect is certainly true with AO questions. To help you sharpen your visual acuity, here are some tougher questions to practice with.

1. In the following diagram, which figure best shows how the objects in the first box would touch if points A and B were connected?

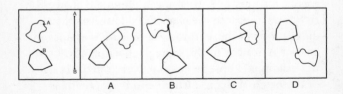

2. Which answer choice best shows how the objects in the first box would appear if they were fitted together?

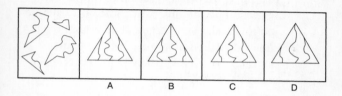

3. In the following diagram, which figure best shows how the objects in the first box would touch if points A and B were connected?

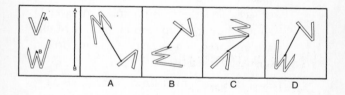

4. Which answer choice best shows how the objects in the first box would appear if they were fitted together?

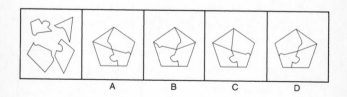

Answers and Explanations

1. **D.** Choices A and C have one connector placed on the wrong section of one of the objects. The top object in choice B is rotated too much and at an angle. The example shows that the line must attach to point A straight on. This makes D the correct answer.

2. **C.** The shapes in answers A and D are not the same size as those the example. Answer B contains mirrored images.

3. **A.** Choices B and C have one connector placed on the wrong section of one of the objects, plus the *W* is mirrored. Answer D shows the right connection, but the letters are mirrored. That leaves A as the correct answer.

4. **A.** The shapes in answers B and C don't match the example. In answer D, all the pieces are mirrored.

Resources

Tons of great resources out there can help you prepare for the ASVAB overall, as well as give you practice in the subject areas of the individual subtests. We recommend checking out the following books and websites:

Air Force website: www.airforce.com

Army website: www.goarmy.com

Careers in the Military.com: www.careersinthemilitary.com

Coast Guard website: www.uscg.mil

Dennis, Johnnie T., and Gary F. Moring. *The Complete Idiot's Guide to Physics*. Indianapolis: Alpha Books, 2006.

DePree, Christopher. *The Complete Idiot's Guide to Astronomy*. Indianapolis: Alpha Books, 2001.

Guch, Ian. *The Complete Idiot's Guide to Chemistry*. Indianapolis: Alpha Books, 2006.

How Stuff Works.com: www.howstuffworks.com

Kelley, W. Michael. *The Complete Idiot's Guide to Algebra*. Indianapolis: Alpha Books, 2007.

Lynn, Vyvyan, and Tony Molla. *The Complete Idiot's Guide to Auto Repair*. Indianapolis: Alpha Books, 2007.

Marine Corps website: www.marines.com

Merriam-Webster's Word of the Day: www.merriam-webster.com/cgi-bin/mwwod.pl

Miller, Steve. *The Complete Idiot's Guide to the Science of Everything.* Alpha Books, 2008.

Military.com website: www.military.com

Military Entrance Processing Command website: www.mepcom.army.mil

Navy website: www.navy.com

Prefixsuffix.com: www.prefixsuffix.com

Seifert, Mark F. *The Complete Idiot's Guide to Anatomy Illustrated.* Indianapolis: Alpha Books, 2008.

Stradley, Laura, and Robin Kavanagh. *The Complete Idiot's Guide to the ASVAB.* Indianapolis: Alpha Books, 2010.

Szecsei, Denise. *The Complete Idiot's Guide to Geometry.* Indianapolis: Alpha Books, 2007.

The Official Site of the ASVAB Testing Program: www.official-asvab.com

Today's Military.com: www.todaysmilitary.com

Index

T